Spain

A CULINARY ROAD TRIP

An Imprint of HarperCollinsPublishers

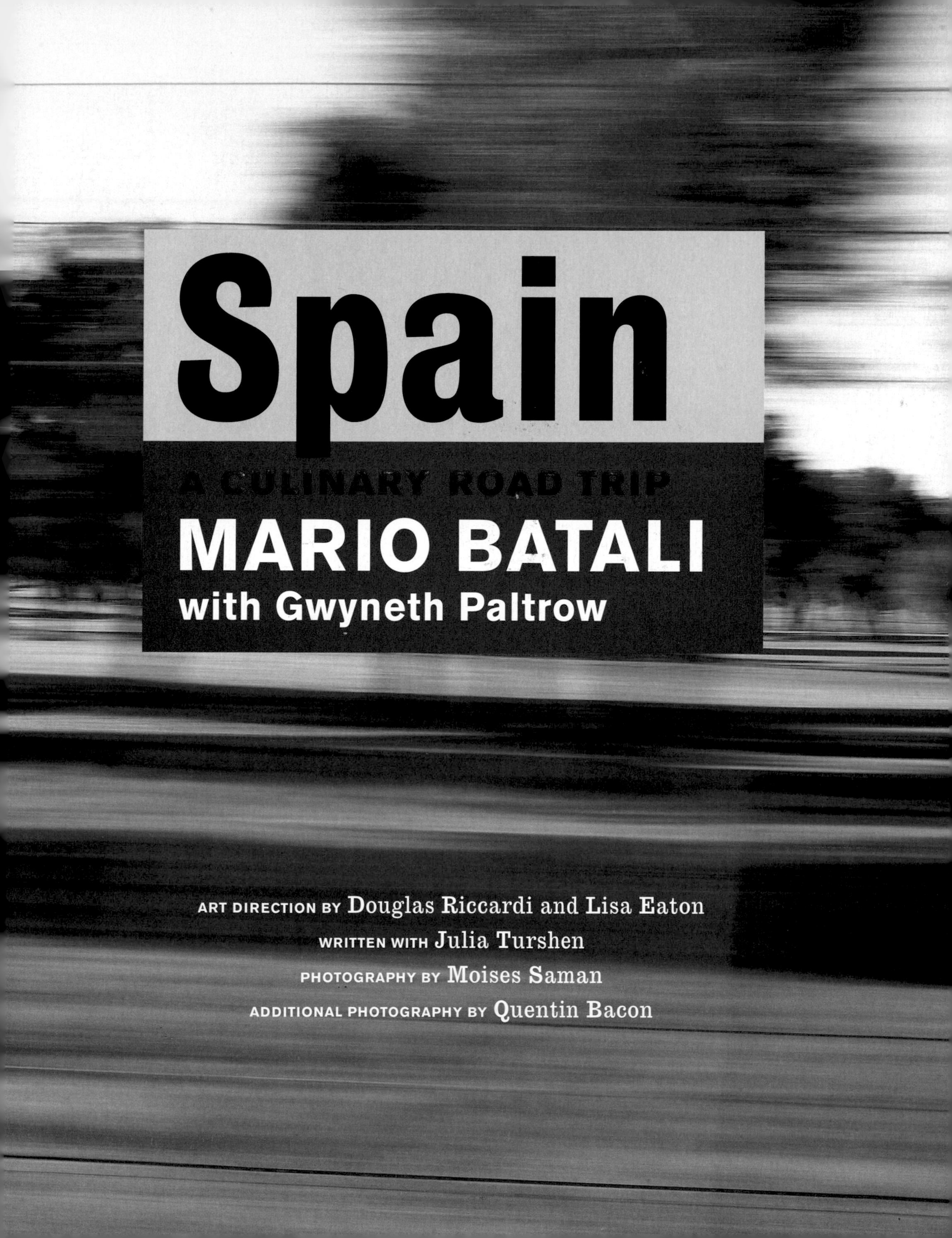

Spain

A CULINARY ROAD TRIP

MARIO BATALI

with Gwyneth Paltrow

ART DIRECTION BY Douglas Riccardi and Lisa Eaton

WRITTEN WITH Julia Turshen

PHOTOGRAPHY BY Moises Saman

ADDITIONAL PHOTOGRAPHY BY Quentin Bacon

All photography © 2008 by Moises Saman, except for the photographs on pages
148–149, 156–162, 164–166, and 170–171, which are © 2008 by Xavier Garcia i Marlii;
and the photographs on pages 24, 29, 39, 50–51, 53, 59, 70, 73, 82, 85, 100, 119, 139,
153, 169, 184, 192, 197, 207, 212, 234, 237, 250–251, 266, 269, 282, 310–311, 327–329,
338, 341–342, 345, and 347; which are copyright © 2008, by Quentin Bacon.

HarperCollins books may be purchased for educational, business, or sales promotional
use. For information, please write: Special Markets Department, HarperCollins
Publishers, 10 East 53rd Street, New York, NY 10022.

ISBN: 978-0-06-156093-4

FIRST EDITION

08 09 10 11 12   /RRD   10 9 8 7 6 5 4 3 2 1

Designed by Memo Productions, NY

Library of Congress Cataloging-in-Publication Data is available upon request.

To Susi, Benno, and Leo. The most delightful and tasty parts of the paella of my life.

— MARIO

Para mi familia, los amores de mi vida.
Y para la familia Lázaro, mi otra familia, la gente
que abrieron la puerta y mi corazón a España.

— GWYNETH

I WOULD LIKE TO THANK THE FOLLOWING:

First and foremost, **SUSI**, **BENNO**, **AND LEO**, for their constant support and love; without them, I simply would not exist

GWYNETH PALTROW, for her faultless palate and fabulous sense of humor on the road again

CHARLIE PINSKY, for the Zen-master-meets-commando approach to making this show and this book a reality of ethereal beauty and deliciousness

SAM SHINN, **DON BARTO**, **PETER MCENTYRE**, **AND GARY GRIFFIN**, for driving up and down and backwards to capture the images and sound in a way I have never seen before

MOISES SAMAN for his moody still images and soft shoulder

ERIC RHEE and the entire crew at **PINSKY PICTURES**—Terry Abbott, Kristian Arija, Tomás Bernar, Maria Carrera, Sergio De La Fuente, Sam Gerstein, Emily Graham, Ramiro Hernandez, Ciona Johnson, Daniel Mayo, Bartolo Perez, Alexandra Rickards, Darren Ridley, and Adam Vardy—for creating great vibes and great TV on a daily basis

MARK BITTMAN, for his sharp mind and infallible sense of taste

CLAUDIA BASSOLS, for her bright smile and love of *jamón*

LISA EATON, for constant thought and beauty

DOUGLAS RICCARDI and Memo Productions, for the real throwdown on every page

JULIA TURSHEN, for following every bite, every snack, and every beverage and getting them on a page, and for recipe testing

JUDITH SUTTON, for her clarity and style

QUENTIN BACON, **KRISTA RUANE**, **AND LISA SCHOEN**, for beauty on the plate

DANIEL HALPERN, **EMILY TAKOUDES**, and the whole **ECCO** crew, for their support and wisdom

THE FOLLOWING AUTONOMÍAS, for their help and finance: Comunidad de Madrid, Comunitat Valenciana, Comunidad Autónoma del País Vasco, Comunidad Autónoma del Principado de Asturias, Comunidade Autónoma de Galicia, Generalitat de Catalunya, Govern de les Illes Balears, Comunidad Autónoma de Andalucía, Comunidad Autónoma de Castilla-La Mancha, and Comunidad Autónoma de Castilla y León

THE FOLLOWING SPONSORS, for their support: TURESPAÑA, Freixenet, Chipotle, Pompeian and the *New York Times*

LATIENDA.COM, for the plates

MIGUEL SANZ, for Madrid on a plate

EDUARDO GARCÍA, for pure strength in fighting the lions

My partner, **JOE BASTIANICH**, for pushing forward in our business world in the smartest way

CHEF JOAN OLIVES I MERCADAL, who has sadly passed on, but is still to be trusted

ALL OF THE EMPLOYEES at our restaurants, whose constant drive and hard work allow me the privilege and time to work outside the restaurants too

España, la verdadera y la sabrosa

(Spain, *the true and delicious one*)

A CORUÑA **3**

SANTIAGO de COMPOSTELA **3**

COVADONGA **10**

SAN SEBASTIÁN **5**

ASTURIAS

OVIEDO **10**

CANTABRIA

BILBAO **4**

LUGO **2**

PAÍS VASCO
(BASQUE COUNTRY)

ELCIEGO **4**

NAVARRA

CAMBADOS **3**

VITORIA **5**

GALICIA

LA RIOJA

CASTILLA Y LEÓN

VALLADOLID **8**

RIBERA DEL DUERO **2**

SALAMANCA **8**

SEGOVIA **8**

MADRID **1 / 12 / 13**

ÁVILA **2**

MADRID

CONSUEGRA **1**

— Mark Bittman —

TEMBLEQUE **2**

TOLEDO **1**

EXTREMADURA

CASTILLA-LA MANCHA

CÓRDOBA **7**

MURCIA

— Gwyneth Paltrow —

ANDALUCÍA

— Claudia Bassols —

GRANADA **7**

FIGUERES 9
ROSES 9
VIC 9
PENEDES 6
CATALUNYA
GIRONA 6
ARAGÓN
SANT POL DE MAR 6
BARCELONA 6 / 9
SANT CARLES DE LA RÀPITA 9
OMUNIDAD
ALENCIANA
VALENCIA 12
MENORCA 11
MALLORCA 11
ISLAS BALEARES

— Mario Batali —

CONTENTS

SPAIN & ME

I was born in Seattle, and my family is Italian-American with some French-Canadian thrown in, but I got my true food and wine PhD while living in Spain during my high school years. My dad worked for Boeing and had the opportunity and vision to move the whole family to post-Franco Madrid in 1975. So, effectively, I spent much of my formative gastronomic years traveling around the Iberian peninsula visiting every single church, winery, and *parador* (a national chain of hotels, often located in ancient buildings) with my brother, sister, mom, and dad. That's how we spent our weekends, and it's how we came to love Spain.

Flash forward thirty years: I have two Spanish restaurants in New York, in addition to six Italian ones, plus three more restaurants in Las Vegas and two in Los Angeles. But I must say that my truest roots in the world of food are still deep within the heart of Castile, where my family traveled simply but comfortably, with a constant eye on the best place for a *tortilla española* (the famous potato omelet) or a *pincho moruno* (a small skewer loaded with paprika-marinated meat). We dined everywhere and anywhere, from the classic tapas bars to a country inn with only roast suckling pig on the menu. In the seventies, Spanish food was the simplest in all of Europe, but the distinct, classic regional dishes were always based on

olive oil and garlic. In Valencia, there was paella; in Madrid, *cocido* (a restorative stew of garbanzo beans and cured meats); in Galicia, *fideos* (small pieces of pasta cooked like rice) and *berberechos a la plancha* (small, delectable clams cooked on a hot flat griddle). There was every kind of restaurant, from stand-up-and-only-a-griddle places to elegant dining rooms and *asadores* (places that specialize in roasted meats) of all types. In the last decade or so, Spain has become the leader of the avant-garde world of molecular gastronomy and high-end cutting-edge cooking, a cuisine filled with foamy sauces, experimentation, and provocation. Yet as much as I love and am intrigued by the new style, it is the time-honored classic cooking of Spain that I return to, the dishes built on the spectacular indigenous ingredients that have been the hallmarks of the true *cocina española* (Spanish kitchen) for centuries.

SPAIN & US

So how is it that I set out on a road trip with Gwyneth Paltrow, Mark Bittman from the *New York Times*, and Spanish actress Claudia Bassols? A couple of years ago, I took a long weekend trip to Italy to be a guest on Mark's PBS show *The Best Recipes in the World*. The producer Charlie Pinsky, the crew, and Mark and I traveled SWAT-team style in a couple of vans and a sedan from Rome to Tuscany and back, herded a few Chianina cows around a field, and grilled some five-pound *fiorentina* (Florentine-style) steaks. Mark and I hit it off like Astaire and Rogers, or perhaps I should say Starsky and Hutch, and we knew that we could do some good television together and have a good time as well. Charlie, who has loved Spain his entire life, had always wanted to do a show about Spanish food and culture, and he thought that my Spanish experiences and passion for all things food, wine, cooking, and culture would make me a great candidate for bringing Spain to the United States in a easy, fun, but informed way. Soon after Mark and I signed on, I brought up the idea of the show at a dinner party in Manhattan and Gwyneth, one of my tablemates, immediately expressed interest in participating. She too had spent some time in Spain during her high school years, and she'd maintained close family ties with her "adopted" family (she really surprised me when she began to speak perfect Castilian on the spot). I ran the idea of her participation by Charlie, who loved it, so I arranged a meeting with the three of us, and boom: *Spain . . . on the Road Again*, our television series, was almost set to go. We realized that two New York City dudes and an Academy Award–winning actress traveling around together might make an odd threesome for a television shoot; we needed a fourth player to make the show more dynamic, and we thought it'd be good to have a real Spaniard on our team. Charlie introduced us to none other than actress Claudia Bassols, a bright Catalan bombshell fluent in six languages.

Cut to Madrid in the first week in October 2007, where we hold a press conference and introduce the show to the Spanish media in a sweet little garden at the Santo Mauro Hotel. That evening, the four of us all sit down and get to know each other better over a nice dinner at Casa Lucio, a Madrid hot spot. All of the pieces of the puzzle fit together perfectly. Bittman's curmudgeonly play will be an excellent foil for my constant joy—and, like me, he will eat anything. Gwyneth, who I knew would be perfect in her worldly genius and love for food and history and art, is enthusiastic, curious, and not afraid to ask questions. Claudia, who we all expected to be the Spain expert, reveals she hasn't been to most of the places on our itinerary, so she's unbelievably eager to get going. The trip is set, and the players are *perfectos*.

We put *Spain: A Culinary Road Trip* together to show you where we went and to offer a bit of insider information, along with great recipes and some pretty funny stories. Much like the trip itself, the book incorporates an eclectic selection of incredible people (cheese makers, chefs, architects, and more), memorable meals, engaging history, and a bit of the dialogue that transpired among the four of us. We had as much fun capturing the trip on paper as we did experiencing it. Now, just by flipping a page, you too can hit the road.

A NOTE TO THE READER:

 Throughout this book, you'll find a number of boxes titled "¿Qué es?" Roughly translated, "*Qué es?*" means "What's that?" (there are also a few boxes called "¿Quién es?"—"Who's that?"). It's our way of highlighting all the fun and interesting (although somewhat random) stuff we found along the way.

"WHAT WE'RE EATING": At the beginning of each chapter is a list of the food we ate in the corresponding locations. Each dish written in capital letters refers to a specific recipe. Happy cooking!

I

From MADRID to TOLEDO

WHERE WE'RE GOING

We begin our trip, appropriately enough, in Madrid, Spain's capital. We drink a bit and eat a lot and begin to get to know each other. Then we all head slightly south to Toledo, where we eat and drink a bit more and also meet a great chef. Gwyneth and I meet a wonderful historian who invites us to view El Greco in a new way. Mark and Claudia bounce over to Consuegra, where the famous windmills of Don Quijote spin.

WHAT WE'RE EATING

Huevos Estrellados, Callos, Percebes, Gambas, Churros, PISTO MANCHEGO p. 25, ARROZ CON VERDURAS Y AZAFRÁN p. 26, PARTRIDGE COOKED TWO WAYS p. 27, TORRIJAS p. 28, dinner at Adolfo's, MIGAS p. 38, ROASTED RED PEPPERS p. 38

MADRID

Madrid sits in the geographic center of Spain. It's also a political center, an economic center, and a cultural one. The sixteenth-century Hapsburg monarchs were the first to call Madrid their capital, and ever since then the city has drawn artists and intellectuals, politicians, and even a good chef or two. The city's energetic style—some might call it electric—is addictive. In a single day, you can look at Velazquez's *Las Meninas* in the Prado museum and then at Picasso's *Guernica* in the Reina Sofia museum, take in a bullfight at the Las Ventas bullring, and stop for a snack at a *churrería* (a shop that churns out *churros*, Spain's gift to the world of fried food). It's a city that rewards an enthusiastic outlook—and a certain amount of stamina.

And in 1975, the year that Franco died, the Batalis came. Everything I learned in high school and during my early critical thinking life has Madrid in its backdrop. Returning now to Madrid, after so many years, the first thing I see on walking out of the Hotel Santo Mauro and turning to the right onto Paseo del Prado is the magnificent Plaza de Cibeles. Then there's Plaza Colón and the whole of Madrid comes slamming back to me. I grab a quick *café cortado* (a small dark coffee with a kiss of milk) at one of the many streetside park cafés, sit down with my map, and start to feel as if I never left. This city is, to use local slang, *muy chula,* which translates roughly as "cool," not in terms of temperature, but as a measure of hipness.

· RESTAURANT ·
CASA LUCIO
· MADRID ·

MARK:
We are in Casa Lucio, a place where the owner is old enough to wear a white jacket without irony.

We head out to dinner to a classic old-guard hipster joint called Casa Lucio and enjoy a great first meal together as travelers. Lucio himself is proud to let us know that anyone and everyone from singers to kings come here all the time. He brings us a plate or two of eggs fried in olive oil with soggy fries—and the crowd goes wild! The euphoria of the trip's start has everyone dancing in the shadow of the emperor's new clothes, for a moment at least. Next a plate of *callos* (Madrid's famous stewed tripe dish). It's a faithful rendition, if lacking in any real excitement, but we are in Madrid and so *callos* are good. Next a plate of perfect *percebes* (gooseneck barnacles), and the buzz starts to work for me. *Gambas a la plancha* (shrimp cooked on a hot griddle), and now we are talking the good stuff. Lucio comes back for several more visits, and at some point a big-faced dude introduced as a major flamenco singer joins us. As the evening wanes, we head back to the hotel for a good night's sleep before the start of our magnificent trip.

¿QUÉ es? **HUEVOS ESTRELLADOS**: The most unusual dish at Casa Lucio was *huevos estrellados*. It consists of blond French fries, medium-thick cut, with fried eggs on top. The potatoes, as explained to us by Lucio, are cooked in olive oil. Mark says, "You'd love it if you grew up with it; you can appreciate it as a visitor."

LUCIO:
Everyone has eaten here but the Pope; he's too busy.

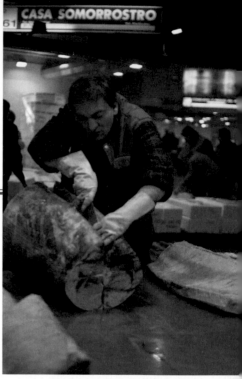

MARK: Any further instructions, General Patton?

MARIO: Yes, Professor Bittman. The most important thing here is to remain in control.

MARK: We shall be in charge of the vehicle.

MARIO: Gwyneth is going to want to drive and want to go to a dress factory or something.

Mark and I get up early, very early, to check out Mercamadrid. It's a pretty unbelievable market. It's huge and industrial, and there are different buildings for each food group. We've come mainly to see the fish, but first we need a little pick-us-up, so we stop at the workers' cafeteria. It looks like a church basement, littered with napkins and sugar packets. It's smoky and the only light is fluorescent. Since it's about 6 a.m., most of the men—and everyone, it seems, is a man—are having a shot or two of *orujo* (Spain's version of grappa) or brandy to end their day. We have *cortados* in glass tumblers and a couple of cold, greasy *churros*.

Then we head into the fish market, which could almost be a huge airport hangar. Men wearing big heavy boots and wielding gigantic knives briskly hack the heads off humongous swordfish and tuna, cleanly fillet white fish, and carefully arrange *gambas* (shrimp) on mounds of ice. We walk around, pointing at the things we like, asking about the things we don't know, and then head back to bed for another hour or two.

While Bittman and I survey the market, the women stay in the hotel and eat *churros*, the fried pieces of pastry perfection that have an extremely crunchy exterior and beg to be dunked into thicker-than-thick hot chocolate. Girls will be girls.

GWYNETH: A big bowl of greasy deep-fried dough to suck up all the alcohol … but they're so good. You're not even hungry, and then you eat one *churro*, and then you want ten.

TOLEDO

ncircled by the Río Tajo, Toledo feels naturally protected. This innate sense of security has made the city Spain's spiritual capital, and its people with their different beliefs have been not only secure, but even celebrated. Toledo has received a variety of inhabitants through the ages, among them the Romans, who arrived in 192 BC; the Visigoths, who came in the sixth century; and the Moors, who settled there in the eighth century.

From as early as 815, and up until the 1080s, Toledo thrived in an atmosphere of *convivencia*, or coexistence. It was one of the few places where Moors, Jews, and Christians lived together in what seems to have been a marriage based purely on commerce but veiled as religious tolerance. Alfonso VI conquered the city in the 1080s, when Toledo was best known for its institutions of law, philosophy, culture, and medicine. Even after Alfonso VI's conquest, both Jews and Moors enjoyed intellectual and commercial freedom until their eventual expulsions, in 1492 and 1502 respectively.

ADOLFO MUÑOZ

First day of driving on the road trip starts with a bang . . . thunder, that is. Rain is definitely on the plain in Spain. Gwyneth is at the wheel and we cruise slowly out of Madrid and into the country. We are just getting used to the new car when Gwyneth pushes a button and begins to vibrate; she says that the seat is bugging out and so is she. Luckily she locates the button for the self-massaging seat, and we can once again concentrate on the Spanish countryside.

Our destination, the spectacular home and bodega of Adolfo Muñoz, is, essentially, *my dream house.* Adolfo owns both this and the best restaurant in town, and he is considered among Spain's top fifty chefs. He's a cool, wired dude with a nice staff, sharp kids, and a beautiful wife all in support. The rain stops for a moment, and we decide to cook outside and set up a grill on the patio. Out of nowhere, a gale-force wind blows in with a flash flood of rain and wind, and all hell breaks loose in our kitchen under a canopy. But then, like a miracle, the clouds go away and two rainbows come out.

Adolfo offers to teach Gwyneth a Spanish way of cooking rice, and then he shows us how to make *pisto* and *perdiz*, partridge (which also spells the end-of-the-gastrointestinal-road for yours truly). But before my downfall, he shows us an unconventional version of one of the most delicious desserts, *torrijas*—bread soaked in red wine (usually *torrijas* involve a lot of milk), dipped in egg, deep-fried, and then sprinkled with cinnamon and sugar. The food is all new to me, and that doesn't happen too much anymore.

We end our visit with a great birthday dinner for Claudia which Adolfo prepares and hosts (see page 30). He is centered, focused, and maybe a little extracaffeinated, but fun to hang with and learn from.

 ¿QUÉ es? **BODEGA**: Apparently my travel companions, all New Yorkers, think a *bodega* is a convenience store. Not in Spain! Here *bodega* refers to a kind of wine warehouse, a huge storage facility. Every vineyard we visited had one and, if we were lucky, let us take a look and maybe even a sip. —**CLAUDIA**

CIGARRAL: Adolfo's vineyard is named Viñedos Cigarral Santa María. The word *cigarral* is a Toledan term that refers to a fenced-in garden outside of a house and comes from *cigarra*, the Spanish word for "cicada."

RECIPE

PISTO MANCHEGO

This simple dish, a sort of pureed ratatouille, is served all over Spain on its own or accompanying meats, eggs, fish, or bread (basically anything and everything).

**SERVES 4 TO 6 AS A TAPA
OR SIDE DISH**

4 ripe plum tomatoes

2 small Japanese eggplants

4 red bell peppers

2 tablespoons olive oil plus ¼ cup

2 red onions, not peeled

Kosher salt and freshly ground
    black pepper

Rub the tomatoes, eggplants, and peppers with the 2 tablespoons of oil and put them on a baking sheet, along with the onions. Roast in a 375°F oven for about 45 minutes, or until very soft (the onions may take as long as an hour). Allow to cool for 10 minutes, then remove the skin from the tomatoes and peel the onions. Cut the eggplants in half and scoop out the flesh. Roughly chop all the vegetables, then pass through a food mill into a bowl. Stir in the remaining ¼ cup olive oil and season to taste with salt and pepper. Serve on *pan tostado* (toasted bread).

ARROZ
con verduras y azafrán

This rice with vegetables and saffron, which Adolfo made for us, was so simple and absolutely tasty. It's kind of like risotto, but, unlike a risotto, it begins by combining the raw rice with stock or water, without first sautéing the rice in olive oil; the oil only comes in at the end of the recipe as an enriching and flavoring addition.

SERVES 6 TO 8 AS A SIDE

1 tablespoon saffron threads

8 cups vegetable stock

2 cups bomba rice
 (you can substitute Arborio)

½ cup finely diced carrot

½ cup finely diced red bell
 pepper

½ cup finely diced peeled turnip

½ cup minced green garlic
 or scallions

½ cup ½-inch-dice asparagus

½ cup ½-inch-dice
 cremini mushrooms

½ cup ½-inch-dice zucchini

½ cup olive oil

A few sprigs of fresh thyme and
 lavender, leaves only

Rosemary blossoms (optional)

Coarse sea salt

Combine the saffron and 1 cup water in a small saucepan, bring to a simmer, and simmer for a few minutes to infuse the water. Heat the stock in a medium saucepan; keep warm over low heat.

Pour the saffron mixture into a large sauté pan, add the rice, and bring to a boil over high heat. Cook, stirring, until the rice has absorbed most of the liquid. Add a generous cup of the vegetable stock, the carrot, pepper, and turnip and bring to a simmer, then reduce the heat slightly and cook, stirring, until most of the stock has been absorbed. Continue to cook, stirring and adding stock each time the previous addition has been absorbed, for about 18 minutes, or until the rice is barely al dente. Add the remaining vegetables and about 1 cup more stock (you may not need all the stock) and cook, stirring, until the vegetables are tender and the rice is perfectly cooked, about 5 minutes longer. Remove from the heat and stir in the olive oil. Spoon into deep bowls and sprinkle with the thyme, lavender, optional rosemary blossoms, and a generous pinch of sea salt.

PARTRIDGE
cooked two ways

Adolfo likes to prepare his partridge breasts on the rare side…the very rare side. During our cooking lesson, Gwyneth warned me that I was about to eat partridge sushi, but I figured I should try everything at least once in life. Little did I know that this decision would lead to a night of intestinal suffering and that it would become part of a story that Gwyneth would return to over and over again during the road trip. For the record, an internal temperature of 155°F in the breast and 170°F in the thickest part of the thigh will allow you to safely enjoy a succulent bird.

SERVES 6 AS A MAIN COURSE

6 partridges

1 large bunch thyme

6 fresh bay leaves, plus a few leaves for garnish

2 tablespoons black peppercorns

20 roasted garlic cloves (see Note)

2 cups dry white wine

Olive oil

Kosher salt and freshly ground black pepper

Using a sharp knife, cut the legs from the partridges. Slice the breasts from the bone. Refrigerate the legs and breasts. Put the partridge carcasses in a stockpot and add the thyme (reserve a few sprigs for garnish), bay leaves, peppercorns, garlic, white wine, and enough water to cover the bones. Bring to a simmer, skimming frequently, then reduce the heat and simmer very gently for 6 hours, skimming often and adding more water as necessary.

Strain the stock into a medium pot, bring to a boil, and reduce by half, to about 2 cups. Add the partridge legs, reduce the heat, and simmer for 20 minutes, or until cooked through. Meanwhile, rub the partridge breasts with olive oil, season with salt and pepper, and grill over a hot fire until cooked to your liking. Thinly slice the breasts and serve alongside the legs, garnished with thyme and bay leaves.

NOTE: For the roasted garlic, slice off the top ⅓ inch or so of 2 garlic bulbs, exposing the cloves. Drizzle with a little olive oil, wrap in foil, and roast in a 350°F oven for 1 hour, or until the cloves are soft. Let cool, then separate the cloves and squeeze them out of their skins.

RECIPE

TORRIJAS

GWYNETH: It smells like Wonder Bread, but in a good way.

MARIO: Fried bread soaked in wine . . . dangerous. It's like French toast meets bruschetta meets red wine, written by Cervantes somewhere in La Mancha.

SERVES 6

3 cups olive oil

2 cups dry Spanish wine

Eighteen ½-inch-thick slices
    crusty Spanish bread
    (or substitute a baguette)

3 large eggs

¼ cup sugar, mixed with 2 tsp.
    ground cinnamon

Mosto (see box below)

Heat the olive oil in a large heavy pot over medium-high heat until it reaches 365°F. Meanwhile, pour the wine into a large shallow bowl, add the bread, and let soak briefly, until evenly moistened. In another shallow bowl, beat the eggs until well mixed. Working in batches, remove the bread from the wine, draining well, add to the eggs, and turn to coat on both sides, then add to the hot oil and cook until golden brown, about 1 minute per side. Drain on paper towels, sprinkle with the cinnamon sugar, drizzle with mosto, and serve to friends.

¿QUÉ es? **MOSTO**: *Mosto* is a Spanish term that refers to unfermented grape juice. Mosto is often cooked to reduce it, but it can be used in its raw state during harvest times. To mimic this at home, boil 3 cups of dry red wine with 1 cup sugar, a cinnamon stick, and a splash of fresh apple cider until it is reduced by three-quarters (it will be thick and syrupy). Allow it to cool, then store it in a clean wine bottle. Use whenever you need a sweet, grapey punch, in everything from a salad dressing to an ice cream topping.

CLAUDIA'S BIRTHDAY DINNER

Adolfo makes a delicious and beautiful series of courses for Claudia's birthday dinner. First are rare mackerel, then shrimp with baby onions and vegetables. Next are gorgeous little *chipirones* (baby squid) with *pisto* (a roasted vegetable puree) and then *arroz con perdiz* (rice with partridge—luckily, perfectly cooked partridge). To finish, a beautiful *torta a la nata* (a cream cake). We drink white wine straight from Adolfo's vineyards and Claudia, who tends to limit herself to a glass of wine or two for a whole meal, drank, as well she should, as if there were no tomorrow.

GWYNETH: Did you just say that you don't like truffle oil? How is that possible?

MARIO: Because truffle oil is made at the same place where they make Chanel No. 5. They don't make truffle oil from truffles; it's fabricated.

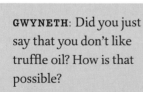

MARK: It's illegal, it's an illegal wine!

All over Europe, there are rules and regulations about the amount of land that can be planted with grapes and the kinds of grapes growers can plant. This is to prevent a glut of low-quality wine created with homogenized varietals. Adolfo had planted some Chardonnay vines in his yard but was then informed by someone in the EU wine version of the Keystone Cops that the vines were not legal according to code. But he made the wine before removing the offending vines, and damn!—it was good. There are probably a couple hundred bottles of this wine left in his home cellar, and then it will be gone forever, the elusive barrel-aged Chardonnay of Toledo.

RUFINO MIRANDA

We meet Rufino Miranda in Toledo outside the Iglesia de Santo Tomé, where El Greco's *El Entierro del Conde de Orgaz* (The Burial of the Count of Orgaz) hangs. Rufino is eighty-five years old and has lived in many different parts of the world, but he now proudly calls Toledo home. He is the local historian and attributes his intelligence and wisdom to his age. "The Devil, *el diablo*, is very wise not because he's the Devil," he says, "but because he's old." Rufino is a kind, passionate, and patient teacher and his enthusiasm for history and art is infectious.

EL GRECO PAINTING

Born in Crete, El Greco (The Greek) lived in Toledo for the latter part of his life. Painted between 1586 and 1588, *El Entierro del Conde de Orgaz* is a dreamy example of the artist's crazy mannerist way with human figures. The childlike soul of Gonzalo Ruiz, Count of Orgaz, enters a nearly abstract heaven inhabited by elongated figures through a fuzzy and surreal womb. Having the confidence to leave a traditional and figurative contemporary Earth behind for more intangible realms was a recurring theme in El Greco's most famous works.

RUFINO: I see the painting as divided in half horizontally. It's spiritual on the top and physical on the bottom. I think I am the same way: I am eighty-five years old and above my waist I am very good, below my waist is a mess.

U nfortunately I couldn't make it to Consuegra, the small town that is home to *los molinos*, the famous windmills Cervantes portrayed in *Don Quijote de la Mancha*. But Mark and Claudia told me all about the endless sky and the somewhat magical light, and Claudia said that with such scenery it was easy to give free reign to imagination and to picture Don Quijote tilting at the windmills.

On their side trip, Mark and Claudia met Juan and Vicente, two carpenters-turned-windmill-restorers who demonstrated the fascinating workings of the old mills. Juan and Vicente are passionate about restoring the windmills and are dedicated to their task. They are hardworking, thoughtful, and brave enough to climb up the windmills every day.

JAVIER MUÑOZ

Mark and Claudia are joined by Javier Muñoz in Consuegra. Javier is one of Adolfo Muñoz's sons and, in addition to being a wine expert, makes a mean plate of *migas*, a traditional dish of the Spanish peasants. Javier sets up a small stove on the hillside near the windmills and teaches Mark and Claudia how to make *migas* with chorizo and pancetta—though it can be made with just about anything so long as bread crumbs are involved. It's a bit like Thanksgiving stuffing and is an incredibly versatile dish.

A NOTE FROM CLAUDIA ON HAM

I eat *jamón*, air-dried Spanish ham, every day, usually for breakfast. The best one we've tried so far was in Madrid. It was called Cinco Jotas and, in Mario's words, it was killer. It was soft and succulent, and it had a really complex flavor.

CLAUDIA: The ingredients are thankful that we are so good to them, and we will be grateful to them quite soon.

RECIPE

MIGAS

This is very good served with eggs fried in olive oil.

**SERVES 6 AS A SIDE DISH
OR TAPA**

6 cups coarse dried bread crumbs

⅓ cup olive oil

6 garlic cloves, not peeled

½ pound Spanish chorizo, casings
    removed and cut
    into ½-inch dice

½ pound pancetta in one piece,
    cut into ½-inch dice

A large bunch of grapes

6 Roasted Red Peppers (recipe
    follows), peeled, seeded,
    and cut into wide strips

Put the bread crumbs in a bowl, sprinkle with just enough water to moisten, and cover with damp paper towels. Set aside for 2 hours, or until the bread is evenly moistened.

Heat the olive oil in a large skillet over medium-high heat. Add the garlic and stir until lightly browned and fragrant, 1 to 2 minutes. Add the chorizo and pancetta and cook, stirring, until the meat is lightly browned and starting to render its fat, about 8 minutes. Add the bread crumbs, mix thoroughly, and cook, stirring, until the crumbs are lightly browned. Serve with the grapes and roasted peppers (peel the garlic cloves if you like, or let your guests do it).

RECIPE

ROASTED RED PEPPERS

The peppers that grow in the region where the windmills are located are deep red and really flavorful. They're often served alongside grilled steaks and even with French fries. Here, served with migas, they add color and sweetness.

SERVES 6 OR MORE

6 red bell peppers

3 tablespoons extra-virgin
    olive oil

Rub the peppers all over with the oil. Grill or broil, turning often, until the skin is blackened all over, about 10 minutes. Let cool, then peel the peppers, rubbing the skin gently to remove all the charred bits. Cut in half and remove the stems and seeds.

After eating *migas* by the windmills, Mark and Claudia go to meet Alfonso Álvarez Valera. Alfonso makes some of the best Manchego cheese in Spain, under the label Artequeso, at Finca La Prudenciana, his artisanal farm dotted with walnut trees, bales of hay piled two stories high, and barking dogs of various sizes.

Mark described the process, which all starts with good milk: Claudia, fearless and frightened at the same time, apparently stepped into the stalls to milk her first sheep and grabbed on without hesitation. Alfonso has 1,200 sheep, whose milk goes into a tank and is stirred with rennet (Claudia's new favorite term) to separate the curds from the whey. After the curds are pressed and washed, they're molded into wheels and then aged in a labyrinthine, wonderfully stinkalicious cave. Plastic crates of the cheese are stacked to the ceiling, and the deeper you go, the stronger the smell.

But the production is only as technologically advanced as it needs to be—the crates are labeled with scraps of notebook paper tied with red ribbon. After aging, some of the cheeses develop a natural mold that is then rubbed with olive oil; others are coated in rosemary. Mark and Claudia spot Pascuala, an expert in coating, spreading wheels of cheese with some green gunk, as if she were frosting cakes. The mixture, it turns out, is a combination of *romero* (rosemary) and *manteca* (lard).

I'LL EAT ANYTHING...
EXCEPT FOR THAT!

GWYNETH:
I DON'T EAT ANIMALS WITH FOUR LEGS.

I'll eat a chicken or a duck that has lived a good, happy life. I'll eat mussels, but I'm with Claudia on the percebes situation. I love bread. I won't eat tripe. I am obsessed with anchoas (anchovies), and I love cheese. I'll eat eggs now and then. Churros con chocolate are wonderful—anything fried, for that matter, is pretty wonderful, especially fried dough, or fried potatoes. I don't know if Spain, and particularly my adopted Spanish father (who raises pigs), will ever forgive me, but I plan on traveling across the country without ever going near what everybody in the world tells me is the best ham.

MARIO:
I eat everything . . . **EXCEPT FOR DURIAN**
(the spiky Asian fruit that smells like a gas-station bathroom in July).

CLAUDIA:
I eat mussels, **BUT NOT PERCEBES**
(which Mark argues taste similar but I argue look very different!). I love shrimp, but just the bodies—not the heads. I am an olive connoisseur. Jamón is my passion—I have it every day of my life. I love it. Olive oil is my other passion, I need it every day of my life. I have never eaten an oyster, nor bull's tail, which is not very Spanish of me. Same for kidneys, brains, and other organ meats. I have a feeling I may be challenged about this along the road trip but, hey, I'm a modern Spanish woman.

MARK:
I WILL EAT ANYTHING. *Anything good.*

WHAT WE'RE LOOKING FORWARD TO

We have a bit of a handle on the center of the country now and decide to head north toward Galicia. No fools, we plan to make a few stops, mostly to eat, on the way. Gwyneth goes home to London for a bit to spend time with her children, but she jumps back into the trip before we can say "jamón."

2

From TEMBLEQUE to LUGO

TEMBLEQUE

From Quintanar de la Orden, the route C402 runs west from Toledo to Templeque, a typical little La Mancha town. It has an attractive seventeenth-century Plaza Mayor that was originally a bullring but is now decked out with three tiers of arcaded galleries, ripe and ready for a gunfight or a vicious beheading with a blood-crazed throng cheering for sangría.

It turns out that our tour guide knows of a great restaurant and Tembleque, besides being a seemingly perfect location to a shoot a Western-style movie, is a great place to stop for lunch. We eat at one of the two places in this 2,271-inhabitant burg and, well, the food is good. We take a few spins around town in the Mercedes and then stop and jump out at a sweet little table set alone in the middle of the plaza and we dine, ah yes, we dine. The *tortilla española* is one of the finest I have had—sweet onions and creamy waxy potatoes really take the eggs up the highway fast; it is moist, but not juicy, and dense, not light, and that is why I love it so. Fried sardines are a picture-perfect *frito* (it is amazing what good clean olive oil in the fryer can do to fish), and we rejoice. The asparagus *a la plancha* is simple enough, though where they got these, I am unsure, as it's not the season. Just enough char to kick the sweetness in with the crunchy mouthfeel, and yet with enough room for the herbal component to totally destroy the thin white wine we started with. But then the waiter brings out the red wine, as if to begin again, and we drink it with a heroically presented *carne a la piedra*, meat cooked on a stone. The provenance of the cut of meat is whispered in hushed tones. Ahh, this is the *secreto*, a butcher's cut from the base of the shoulder; and we will also keep it a secret. The meat is fabulous, deep dark pork from Iberian pigs (whose cured legs have only recently been granted entry into the United States and are available at a cost in a few select markets). The ripples of creamy white fat throughout yield a porky fragrance upon their introduction to the hot *piedra* (stone) and a delightful complexity and succulence upon introduction to our mouths. This is great eating, especially given that we are sitting alone on a virtual movie set in the old bullring.

THE NEIGHBORHOOD KIDS

While we were waiting for lunch to get started, we met Sofía, Anna, and Domingo—local kids around five or six years old. They were eating ice cream and talked about their neighborhood. Domingo is a bit of a character, and he told Claudia how his uncle let him ride a tractor and he got pulled over by the police. She called him *un pequeño delincuente*, a little delinquent.

ASPARAGUS
a la plancha

Pretty much any vegetable—actually, almost anything—can be cooked a la plancha. *A plancha is a hot metal surface, sort of like a super-hot griddle. It's one of the Spanish gifts to the world of cooking. At home, a hot cast-iron skillet is a good substitute.*

SERVES 6

1 pound asparagus, tough
   bottom ends snapped off
2 tablespoons olive oil
Kosher salt
1 lemon, halved crosswise
   and quartered

Heat a *plancha* or a large cast-iron skillet over high heat until very, very hot (this will take a few minutes). Rub the asparagus all over with the olive oil, add to the pan (in batches if necessary), and cook, turning once, until just tender, about 4 minutes. Transfer to a platter, sprinkle with salt, and squeeze over the lemon juice.

CARNE
a la piedra

This is the "secret" cut of pork shoulder, with magnificent ripples of marbling they served us at our lunch in Tembleque. It's a terrifically fun dish, since you cook it yourself on a hot stone on your table. At home, a cast-iron skillet will do just fine. Everyone cooks it to their own liking—Claudia prefers hers well-done, Mark and I beg to differ.

SERVES 4

1 pound boneless pork shoulder, frozen for 30 minutes (this will make it easier to slice)
A 2-ounce chunk of slab bacon
Kosher salt

Heat a large cast-iron skillet over high heat. Meanwhile, slice the pork as thin as possible. Rub the fatty part of the bacon over the hot skillet to lightly grease it, then remove the bacon. Add only as many slices of pork as will fit in a single layer and cook for a minute or less per side, until seared and cooked to your liking. Transfer to a platter and sprinkle with salt. Continue until all the meat is cooked, regreasing the skillet with the bacon as necessary.

FRIED SARDINES

I love tiny fried fish of any type. They're a staple in many cuisines, but they seem to taste better in Spain than anywhere else because they're fried in great Spanish olive oil. Spaniards tend to fry them whole—guts and all—and they're quite good that way. If you'd like to clean them up a little, just make a slit down the fish's belly and remove the innards with your finger under running water.

SERVES 4

6 to 8 cups extra-virgin olive oil, for deep-frying

1 cup all-purpose flour, plus about 1 cup for dredging

1 teaspoon baking powder

1 teaspoon kosher salt

½ teaspoon freshly ground black pepper

1 large egg

1 cup dry white wine

1 pound sardines, cleaned and scaled

Coarse sea salt

Heat 3 inches of oil to 350°F in a large heavy pot. Meanwhile, whisk the flour, baking powder, salt, and pepper together in a large bowl. Whisk the egg and wine together, then whisk into the flour mixture. The batter should be the consistency of thin pancake batter; add a little water if necessary.

Working in batches, dredge the sardines in flour, shaking off the excess, then coat in the batter, letting the excess drip off, and add to the hot oil. Cook until golden, about 5 minutes. Drain on paper towels, sprinkle with salt, and serve hot.

ÁVILA

Ávila, capital of Castilla y León, rests at 3,600 feet above sea level, comfortable in the shelter of the Sierra de Gredos. Its mythic walls screen a distinctive amalgam of Renaissance palaces and churches. The walls stand as a reminder of the city's grand moment, when it was the leading power in the textile industry.

Birthplace of Priscillian, ascetic mystic and perhaps the first suffragist as well as the first Christian martyred as a heretic by the Christians way back in the late fourth century, Ávila is probably better known as the birthplace of Santa Teresa de Jesús. Saint Teresa was a mystic, a major figure in the Catholic Reformation, and a staunch believer in the personal inner world of faith and the potential in belief for ecstasy. Her most famous vision, among many, was of being repeatedly stabbed through the heart with a lance, during which she experienced the ecstasy of suffering. Bernini immortalized her in his famous *Ecstasy of St. Teresa* (in Rome). Ávila has a number of religious buildings—inside and outside the walls—related to the life of the saint.

Ribera del Duero is gaining recognition as one of Spain's best wine regions. This *denominación de origen* (DO) follows the Duero River from an area north of Valladolid, centers on the town of Aranda de Duero, and then meanders eastward through San Esteban Gormaz. It is home to Spain's most famous and expensive wine, Vega Sicilia. Some of my friends produce a few of the great red wines in the area at a winery called Valdubón, in the beautifully hilly, rosemary-scented countryside north of Segovia.

Since we got lost getting to Valdubón, we are starving when we finally arrive. Luckily lunch comes quickly—deep-fried rings of squid, luscious croquettes made with Manchego, inch-thick slices of fried *morcilla* (blood sausage), chorizo, *tortilla española*, and bread with olive oil. We wash it down with *cava* (Spanish sparkling wine) and *vino tinto* (red wine). So satisfying, so Spanish.

Later we set up a grill in the vineyards and prepare baby lamb for dinner. We burn grapevines for fire and squeeze grapes over the meat. Then we eat it with Valdubón wine: a totally integrated, inclusive meal.

 ¿QUÉ es? **MORCILLA**: *Morcilla* is a sausage made of rice, fresh pigs' blood and fat, cumin, pepper, and onions—stuffed into casings, steamed, and then sliced and fried or grilled.

The first time I watched *morcilla* being made was when I was in Italy. My mentor, Quintiglio, grabbed a pig by its hind legs with a rope and pulled it upwards; I had no idea what he was doing. The next thing I knew, he had hacked into the pig's neck and collected the blood in a bucket. He ran the bucket of fresh blood into the kitchen, mixed it with rice and onions, and stuffed it into sausage casings. Thirty minutes after the final squeal, we were eating morcilla and bread. I was impressed.

TORTILLA
española

Tortilla española is essentially the national dish of Spain. You can eat it as a tapa, for breakfast, in a bocadillo *(sandwich), or for dinner with salad and a bit of* jamón. *Basically anytime, anywhere. We had a great one at Valdubón and I think it's because they weren't afraid to use a lot of olive oil. No fear!*

SERVES 4 TO 6 AS A TAPA OR APPETIZER

¼ cup extra-virgin olive oil

1¼ pounds waxy potatoes, peeled and thinly sliced

1 medium onion, thinly sliced

8 extra-large eggs

Kosher salt and freshly ground black pepper

Heat the oil in a large cast-iron or nonstick skillet over medium-high until very hot but not smoking. Add the potatoes and onion, season with salt and pepper, reduce the heat to medium, and cook, stirring occasionally and adjusting the heat if necessary so that the vegetables do not brown, until the potatoes are tender when pierced with the tip of a paring knife, 15 to 20 minutes.

Meanwhile, beat the eggs with salt and pepper to taste in a large bowl. Add the potatoes to the eggs, then pour into the skillet, spreading the potatoes evenly in the pan. Cook for about 1 minute, just to set the bottom of the egg mixture. Reduce the heat to medium-low and cook for 20 minutes, or until almost set throughout. Carefully flip the tortilla over (invert it onto a plate if you must, then slide it back into the pan, bottom side up) and cook for 5 minutes longer, until set. Flip out onto a clean plate and allow to rest for 5 minutes. Serve warm or at room temperature.

GRILLED LECHAZO

One of the best things we ate on our trip was lechazo—lamb under twenty-five days old, fed only mother's milk. Its full hanging weight is twelve pounds or less. Lamb this good is a gift from the sweet earth herself.

Preparing lechazo is a great example of less-is-more. When you have a product this good, you want to do as little as possible to it. The best way to procure such a magnificent product is from an equally magnificent butcher. Rub the lamb with some good olive oil and fresh rosemary, maybe some grapes, and throw it on a grill (preferably fired by grapevines, but a gas or charcoal grill will do just fine): it will make the crowd roar!

SERVES 6 TO 8

Several large bunches of dried grapevines

½ lechazo (baby lamb; about 12 pounds), leg separated from the shoulder/rack, boned, and butterflied (you can have the butcher do this), shoulder/rack trimmed if necessary

Kosher salt

1 bunch rosemary

Extra-virgin olive oil

1 bunch ripe tempranillo grapes (or the nearest cluster of grapes)

Start a fire with the grapevines and wait for them to burn down to embers. Sprinkle the lamb with salt, pinch over some rosemary leaves, and drizzle with olive oil. Rub the grapes over the meat, mashing them to release their juice, then discard most of the grape skins. Set two rocks on either side of your fire, lay the remaining rosemary branches over the coals, and place a grilling rack across the rocks so that it is very close to the fire. Grill the lamb until cooked to medium, about 6 minutes per side for the leg, 10 minutes per side for the shoulder/rack. Let rest for about 10 minutes before carving.

GWYNETH: You ate baby lamb! That's such bad karma, eating a baby.

MARIO: Imagine all the tiny little soys that gave their life for your milk.

GRILLED CHULETILLAS

Chuletillas are the tiny little rib chops cut from the lechazo. *About the size of a lollipop, they can be eaten in a single, delicious bite. Grilling them at Valdubón, I incorporated the entire vineyard. The fire was made from grapevines and the lamb was seasoned with some of the grapes, along with rosemary and lavender from bushes that lined the driveway. Here I've provided a more home-friendly recipe, but if your home includes a sprawling vineyard, by all means throw your chuletillas on a smoldering pile of vine clippings.*

SERVES 6

24 chuletillas (baby lamb rib chops)

2 tablespoons olive oil

2 tablespoons red wine vinegar

1 tablespoon sugar

2 sprigs lavender, leaves removed and chopped

2 sprigs rosemary, leaves removed and chopped

Kosher salt

Rub the lamb chops with the olive oil, vinegar, sugar (the sugar will help caramelize the meat as it sears), lavender, and rosemary. Grill or broil for about 2 minutes per side for medium-rare. Transfer to a platter, sprinkle with salt, and enjoy.

1 GRILLED CHULETILLAS • 2 MORCILLA • 3 GRILLED LECHAZO

GALICIA

Galicia, tucked in Spain's northwest corner, is the country's most raw, untamed region. It is not a stop on the way to something, but rather a beginning and end unto itself—a self-contained, foggy, supernatural kind of place. Here is where women break their backs harvesting *almejas* (clams) and men risk their lives for *percebes* (gooseneck barnacles). Indeed, water rules the area, as the Atlantic is a presence present, if not always visible, all over the region. Even the farmyard *horreos* (granaries) must be elevated above the sodden ground.

LUGO

Migrating Celtic herdsman originally settled the ancient town of Lugo, on the banks of the Miño River, centuries ago. The Roman settlement dates to 13 BC and the town's Roman wall, built as a defense, is still standing today. In 715, Moors sacked and burned most of the town, but by the reign of Alfonso III in the 870s, the town had been rebuilt. The Cathedral of Santa María in Lugo, started in 1129 as a copy of its sister in Santiago, was not truly finished until late in the eighteenth century. It is just a hair or two short of the brilliance of Santiago's Cathedral of Saint James.

Today Lugo is considered one of the two most significant capitals of Galician cooking—the other is Santiago—and some of the best restaurants are within the walls of the old city. However, we have decided to keep to the smallest of small towns on this trip, so we head to a tiny little farming community out in the sticks.

Mark, Claudia, and I drive through the mythic fog of Galicia down a nearly mud road to find A Parada das Bestas, a *casa rural* in the middle of nowhere. The description "casa rural" does not do justice to this delightful little country inn run by María Varela and Suso Santiso, a young, energetic, and dedicated couple. They're both originally from Galicia but lived in other Spanish cities and towns before returning. They bought an old farmhouse and painstakingly restored it, and now they live there with their two young children and run it as a spectacular *casa rural* for adventurous but peace-seeking guests. When we arrive, they turn up the jazz and set out thick *tortillas* with peppers, crusty bread, and an unbelievably rich local sheep's-milk cheese, *queso del país*, "cheese of this land."

I snag a few moments of pure sunshine and sneak out to play a round of golf—and the gods are smiling! On the way back, I pick up Gwyneth at the airport and return to the casa rural for a late supper of *pisto* (Spain's version of ratatouille), vegetables with some sheep's cheese, and *pan con tomate*. Then we all head to bed for a nice sleep in a very quiet part of the world.

We get up early for a breakfast prepared in the hearth of an old fireplace and then take a long walk on the Camino de Santiago. The Camino is beautiful as well as evocative of its intense history. We bump into a lot of pilgrims (*peregrinos*), who may be walking for exercise as well as faith. The town is charming and the cathedral is breathtaking. We walk a bit around and peek in and then snag a coffee at the fifteenth-century Hostal del Los Reyes Católicos. While walking, the four of us make a bet as to who can walk the farthest and plan that the winner will cook dinner. Gwyneth and I win by a mile, so María shows us how to make her braised capon, but Gwyneth accidentally turns off the burner. María saves us with a huge cauldron of *caldo gallego* (the classic Galician soup made with white beans, chorizo, and turnip greens), followed by a few shots of *orujo de hierbas* (a Galician liquor with herbs), and we're off to sleep in the cemetery silence again.

¿QUÉ es?

CASA RURAL: A *casa rural* is a rustic form of lodging popular in the Spanish countryside. These small inns are generally family-run, quiet, comfortable, and affordable. Suso and María's A Parada das Bestas is one of the best—great food, great hosts, and a great setting.

A DAY OF FOOD at PARADA DAS BESTAS

BREAKFAST: fresh orange juice, coffee with hot milk that tastes slightly of chocolate and chicory, thick slices of country bread and plain cake, local blackberry jam, and bananas, oranges, and pears

LUNCH: *fideos con almejas* (short pieces of pasta cooked with clams), slices of *pulpo* (octopus) bathed in olive oil with salt and paprika, boiled potatoes drizzled with olive oil, local capon cooked until the skin is lacquered and the flavor is almost of beef stew, and creamy pecan ice cream with caramel that seems to taste of sherry

DINNER: triangular clay bowls of *caldo gallego*, the hearty soup; peasant bread cut into thick slices; greens adorned only with onions and tomatoes; and two local cheeses—actually the same kind, but at different ages—cut into finger-sized pieces

CAMINO DE SANTIAGO

The Camino de Santiago is a walk…a long, long walk! It's a pilgrimage route, dating back to the ninth century, which originally traversed northern Spain, but then expanded into France and beyond. The route culminates at Santiago de Compostela where the remains of Saint James (Santiago) the Apostle are enshrined in the great cathedral. During the Middle Ages, if you completed the rigorous month-long religious pilgrimage, you were ensured a spot in heaven.

A FEW GOOD THINGS TO KNOW:

1. The camino is trafficked by **COWS**. They have the right-of-way.

2. **STONES** marking the way give location and the number of kilometers remaining to Santiago de Compestela. Think of it like a countdown.

3. You'll also see a lot of **SEASHELLS**, because the shell is the symbol of St. James. Many walkers have shells tied to their backpacks or around their necks. A few come through with dogs who carry their own backpacks adorned with shells.

GWYNETH: I love it out here, it's such fresh, crisp air, and the oxygen helps your body relax.

RECIPE

FILLOAS

A fascinating blend of sweet and savory, these crepe-like pancakes, usually served as a snack, made me think of an American pancake-and-bacon breakfast. María was kind enough not only to show us how to make these, but also to make Gwyneth's without the bacon fat (but pork in my dessert makes me a very happy man).

SERVES 4

2 cups all-purpose flour

1½ teaspooons kosher salt

1 cup chicken stock

2 large eggs, beaten

1 cup milk

About 2 tablespoons bacon fat
    or olive oil

Sugar for sprinkling

Whisk together the flour, salt, and stock in a large bowl until smooth. Whisk in the eggs and milk. Let the batter stand for 30 minutes.

Heat a crepe pan or medium nonstick skillet over medium heat. Add just enough bacon fat to coat the bottom of the pan and heat until hot. Pour in ¼ cup batter, tilting the pan to cover the bottom evenly, and pour out any excess. Cook until golden brown on the first side, about 2 minutes. Carefully flip the pancake and cook until lightly browned on the second side. Remove from the pan, sprinkle with sugar, and roll up. Put on a platter, cover to keep warm, and repeat with the remaining batter. Serve hot or at room temperature.

THE BET

MARIO: We'll see who walks the most. What does the winner get?

MARK: The winner gets to cook dinner.

GWYNETH: The winner!?

MARIO: I think it's a good bet, because then we'll be in charge of our destiny gastronomically.

CAPON
grandma-style

Gwyneth and I won the bet against Mark and Claudia, and María taught us how to make the capon that is one of her specialties. It's a deceptively simple recipe because the bird emerges with an incredible depth of flavor. When the capon first hits the pan, it sounds like a party. Serve with boiled potatoes drizzled with olive oil and salt.

SERVES 8 TO 10

¾ cup olive oil

1 bunch Italian parsley, leaves removed and chopped

2 garlic cloves, thinly sliced

1 tablespoon kosher salt

One 10-pound capon cut into 14 pieces: 2 wings; 2 legs; 2 thighs, cut in half; 2 breasts, cut in half; and back, cut in half

1 cup cognac or other brandy

3 cups dry red wine

2 Spanish onions, cut into 8 wedges each

Combine ½ cup of the olive oil, the parsley, garlic, and salt in a blender and zap until smooth. Put the capon in a baking dish or shallow bowl and pour the parsley mixture over it, turning to coat. Cover and marinate at cool room temperature for 2 hours, or for as long as overnight in the refrigerator.

Heat a large heavy pot over medium-high heat, then add the remaining ¼ cup olive oil and heat until hot. Working in batches, add the capon skin side down and cook until deep golden brown on the first side, about 7 minutes. Turn and cook until deep brown on the second side, about 7 more minutes. Return all the capon to the pot, add the cognac, and boil until reduced by half. Add the wine and boil until reduced by one-third. Add the onions and bring to a simmer, then lower the heat to a gentle simmer, cover, and cook for 2 hours, until the meat is almost falling off the bones.

¿QUÉ es? **PIMENTÓN**: *Pimentón* is smoked paprika that can be found in nearly every kitchen in Spain—and should be in yours too. It's full of smoke and strength, wonderfully powerful, and a little fruity. The color of dark rust, it lends a hint of reddish-orange anywhere it goes. There are three types: *picante* (hot), *dulce* (sweet), and *agridulce* (bittersweet), but even the *picante* is not that hot. I keep tins of *picante* and *dulce* in the house at all times.

RECIPE

Gwyneth's
CHINESE DUCK

*Inspired by María's capon, Gwyneth went home and used the same method
but different flavors to cook duck. It was a big hit! Here are her instructions.*

Get a very good organic duck. Cut it into 14 pieces (see Capon Grandma-Style). Prick the
skin all over with a sharp paring knife. Rub with some softened butter that's been mixed with
3 or 4 minced garlic cloves. Sprinkle with ground cloves and black pepper. Brown the duck well
in olive oil in a large heavy pot. Pour off all but a few tablespoons of the fat and add a cup each
of Madeira and sake, some mirin, a sprinkle of sugar, lots of grated fresh ginger, a few crushed
garlic cloves, and 2 star anise. Bring to a boil, then lower the heat to a gentle simmer, cover, and
cook for 3½ hours, or until the duck is very tender. During the last 10 minutes, add soy sauce to
taste. Serve garnished with tons of chopped cilantro and sliced scallions.

CALDO GALLEGO

We couldn't write about Galicia without including a recipe for caldo gallego, the traditional, restorative soup of Galicia. With a little bread, you've got a great meal on your hands. María's version was especially good, and I don't think it's a coincidence that she grows her own greens. This soup is even better the next day.

SERVES 4 TO 6

½ pound thickly sliced pancetta or slab bacon, cut into ¼-inch dice

1 cup dried white beans, soaked overnight in water to cover

1 large onion, cut into ½-inch dice

2 baking potatoes, peeled and cut into ½-inch dice

2 turnips, peeled and cut into ½-inch dice

½ pound Spanish chorizo, casings removed and sliced ¼ inch thick

1 pound turnip greens (or other dark leafy green), stemmed and coarsely chopped

Cook the pancetta in a large heavy pot over medium heat until most of the fat is rendered, 8 to 10 minutes. Drain the beans, add them to the pot, along with enough water to cover them by 2 inches, and bring to a boil. Skim off the foam, then lower the heat and simmer gently, partially covered, for 45 minutes to 1 hour, or until the beans are beginning to soften.

Add the onion, potatoes, and turnips and cook for 20 minutes, or until the vegetables are softened. Add the chorizo and greens and cook for 10 minutes, or until the greens are tender.

¿**QUÉ es?**

GRELOS: *Grelos* are turnip greens. They're slightly bitter—like broccoli rabe—but very tender when braised. They're wonderful sautéed in olive oil with a bit of garlic and are the star in *caldo gallego*. They grow all over Galicia, and you are likely to see patches of the greens in most backyards. **UNTO**: *Unto* is a cured pork belly product, sort of like the Spanish version of pancetta. We couldn't seem to find it anywhere outside of Galicia. There it's used as the base for *caldo gallego* and is why, I think, *caldo gallego* tastes better in Galicia than anywhere else you might be served it.

Batali Family
BLACKBERRY PIE

Wandering down the Camino past the cows and the cowboys, the pilgrims and the hippies, I noticed a virtually untouched bush with my favorite fruit in life, the blackberry. When I was growing up in Seattle, we used to cruise down Dash Point Road and load the station wagon with wild blackberries. We turned some of our haul into jam and pies, then ate the rest plain with vanilla ice cream, to this day my fave dessert in the whole world. We would make a whole mess of pies and freeze them unbaked, then bake them up in the middle of winter and eat them hot, fragrant with the summer's bounty. The berries on the Camino de Santiago were small and sweet/tart, and I loved them.

SERVES 8

FOR THE CRUST

2½ cups all-purpose flour

3 tablespoons sugar

¼ teaspoon salt

1 cup vegetable shortening, chilled

About 5 tablespoons ice water

FOR THE FILLING

4 cups fresh blackberries

½ cup sugar

3 tablespoons all-purpose flour

1 tablespoon fresh lemon juice

1 tablespoon unsalted butter

For the crust, whisk the flour, sugar, and salt together in a bowl. With a pastry blender or two knives, cut in the shortening until the mixture resembles coarse crumbs. Drizzle over 3 tablespoons of the ice water, tossing with a fork to moisten the mixture evenly, then add more water about 1 teaspoon at a time until the dough comes together. Gather it into a ball, wrap in plastic wrap, and chill for at least 30 minutes.

Cut the dough in half. On a lightly floured surface, roll out one half (keep the remaining dough chilled) to a 12½-inch round, and fit it into a 9-inch pie plate. Put the blackberries in a bowl and toss gently with the sugar, flour, and lemon juice. Transfer to the pie shell and dot with the butter. Roll out the second piece of dough to an 11-inch round. Cover the filling with the dough, trim the excess, and crimp the edges with a fork to seal. Cut a few steam vents in the center of the crust. Bake in a 350°F oven for 1 hour, or until the crust is golden brown and the juices are bubbling. Let cool on a rack for at least 15 minutes.

TOP THREE SPANISH FOOD CHOICES

CLAUDIA:

JAMÓN

PAN CON TOMATE
(special Catalan bread with tomato), and

OLIVE OIL
(can olive oil be considered a dish? I like to think so)

GWYNETH:

PAN CON TOMATE Y

ANCHOAS
(anchovies)

ARROZ
(my adopted mom makes a mean paella) and

MANCHEGO CHEESE
(which tastes completely different from Manchego I get in the States)

MARIO:

JAMÓN
(but I am very picky about it)

FIDEOS
*(the short noodles that are browned before
the cooking liquid is added), and*

MARISCOS A LA PLANCHA
(shellfish cooked on a plancha, a hot griddle)

MARK:

JAMÓN

FRIED TINY FISH
(they're so good here because they're fried in olive oil), and

GRELOS
(turnip greens cooked in Galicia with olive oil, garlic, and salt)

WHAT WE'RE LOOKING FORWARD TO

Feeling nourished and energized by our stay at the
casa rural, we're eager to see more of Galicia—especially
its famed shellfish and Santiago de Compostela.

3

From CAMBADOS to SANTIAGO DE COMPOSTELA

WHERE WE'RE GOING

Our stay at A Parada das Bestas with María and Suso was a wonderful introduction to Galicia, a region we are quickly falling in love with. We arrive in Cambados and meet the *mariscadoras*, the incredible women who harvest Galicia's best clams. Gwyneth jets back to her family for a bit and Mark, Claudia, and I explore Santiago de Compestela and its neighboring villages.

WHAT WE'RE EATING

Berberechos, GWYNETH'S CLAMS p. 83, VINEYARD SEA GRILL p. 84,
percebes, EMPANADA p. 94, FISHERMAN'S ESCABECHE p. 98,
OCTOPUS GALICIAN-STYLE p. 101, QUEIMADA p. 102

CAMBADOS

The tidal flat at the edge of Cambados is host to an astonishing gathering ritual. During low tide, women—and it's exclusively women—dig for clams with nothing but a few blunt tools and backbreaking persistence.

Most of the women wear big rubber boots, but some stand barefoot in the few inches of water littered with seaweed and dead clams. Digging with rakes, big spoons, or flat scoops, they collect clams the size of Ping-Pong balls, measuring each one with calipers. Those that make the cut are divided among tins according to size. When high tide approaches, the women finish gathering and pull their loads into shore.

HOW *to* OPEN *a* CLAM *with a* CLAM

One of the women taught me to open a clam using another clam as a clam knife. In short, you take one clam in each hand, holding it with the tips of your fingers, and place the two hinge sides against each other—you'll find that, amazingly, they fit together like two puzzle pieces. Apply a bit of pressure, but not too much, or you will crush the shells, and twist in opposite directions, as if opening a small jar. This motion will cause at least one shell, sometimes both, to open as if pried apart, and the clam inside is now yours to eat. I used this method with *berberechos*, my favorite of the Cambados mollusks.

GWYNETH: This is the definition of "local eating."

MARIO: These are so good! I knew they would be excellent raw.

MARIO: I think it's the chick's job to dig them out. Mark, let me know when you actually get one.

MARK: If it means I get to eat it, you can call me a lady.

GWYNETH: Yeah, you guys aren't supposed to be here, this work is for the ladies.

MARIO: Well then ladies, get to work!

¿QUÉ es?

BERBERECHO: A *berberecho* is a type of clam, but, to me, it is a cross between a scallop and a clam. It has all of a scallop's resilience in the mouth, as well as a scallop's sweetness. At the same time, it has the salinity and succulence of a clam. It can be identified by its striped ridged shell. A cockle is a good substitute, if you must.

VIONTA WINERY

We go from Cambados to Vionta Winery, a breathtaking vineyard planted around an old castle, where the winemakers proudly present us with one-pound oysters. The ladies are having none of them (the oysters, not the winemakers), but Mark and I oblige. There is also a nice lobster and some live and luscious razor clams, but there is no kitchen. So I decide to start a fire of vine clippings and corncobs (to bring just a little more sweetness) on an old stone table and we cook the lobster and clams right there. Then Gwyneth steams us some big round clams with garlic and Albariño, the Galician white wine. Killer!!

GWYNETH'S CLAMS

When we ate at Casa Pintos after meeting the mariscadoras in Cambados, we were inspired by the chef's use of laurel, bay leaves, in the steamed clams. When we got to the Vionta Winery, Gwyneth volunteered to make us her special clams, with enough garlic to clear your sinuses. The healthy slug of Albariño is key.

SERVES 4

2 pounds berberechos or other clams, scrubbed

1 head garlic, cut in half across the bulb

2 or 3 fresh bay leaves

½ bottle Albariño (or other good Spanish dry white wine)

2 tablespoons extra-virgin olive oil

Put everything in a deep skillet, cover tightly, and steam over medium-high heat until the clams open (yes, it's really that easy).

VINEYARD SEA GRILL

Cooking at the vineyard is definitely a lesson in "it goes with what it grows with." Amazing Galician wine, amazing Galician shellfish, amazing Galician landscape—you can't ask for more.

SERVES 4

One 2½-pound lobster

2 pounds razor clams, scrubbed

¼ cup olive oil

2 tablespoons red wine vinegar

Coarse sea salt

½ bunch Italian parsley,
    leaves removed and chopped

2 lemons, halved

To kill the lobster, hold it firmly on a cutting board with its head toward you, plunge a sharp heavy knife into the center of the head, and quickly bring the knife down to the board, splitting the front of the lobster in half; turn it around and cut it completely in half. Drizzle the lobster and clams with half the olive oil and half the vinegar. Place the lobster shell side down over a hot grill fire, then lay the razor clams on the grill. Cook for 8 minutes, then turn and cook for 3 minutes, or until the lobster is opaque throughout and the clams are just cooked. Transfer to a platter, drizzle with the remaining oil and vinegar, and sprinkle with salt and the parsley. Serve with the lemons.

¿QUÉ es?

NAVAJAS: *Navaja* is the Spanish word for both a fighting knife and a razor clam. I'm, of course, more interested in the second definition. These strange-looking mollusks are long, thin clams that usually measure about five inches long. Cook them as you would any other clam. They're especially great prepared on, yes, a hot *plancha*!

MARIO: This is food-wine poetry.

GWYNETH: The wine poetry is working in and of itself. Mario, you have asbestos fingers.

MARK: He hasn't been doing this for forty years for nothing.

MARIO: If there is one thing that I can count on from you, it's your sarcastic morning-coffeeless attitude and the fact that you'll eat anything I make for you all the time. Which is why I love you so much.

MARK: I'm good for that. Even if I had just had lunch, I'd eat all of that seafood you're grilling.

MARIO: Enjoy the lobster, but make sure that you have a taste of the wine, because that's where the heaven really comes. This is when two separate ingredients added together are more than their sum.

CLAUDIA: Wow, you're a genius.

MARIO: I am not a genius, I am praising the sea that gives us the good things that are so easy to cook. It's about place, not technical expertise, and it's delicious.

PERCEBES

*P*ercebes resemble the nasty toes of an alien more than they do a gooseneck, as the English name, gooseneck barnacle, might lead you to believe. If it was a hungry man who first dared to eat a lobster, it was clearly a deranged one who first decided to eat *percebes*. You may count me in among the crowd of said fellows.

Percebes have a hard shell at the top and a foot at the base, and the rest resembles the attachment to a tire's inner tube. When cleaned properly and steamed, they have the delicate rubberiness of a nicely cooked piece of boiled octopus and the odd coppery flavor of a good wild mussel.

Risky business, daring men gather *percebes* from beneath huge Galician cliffs.

SHOPPING AT ZARA

You risk repeating outfits when you sign up for a road trip. Fine by me, but Claudia definitely suffered from a limited wardrobe. Mark kindly and bravely offered to take her to Zara, the famous Spanish clothing store. Many hours and outfits later, Claudia left with a new wardrobe; Mark left carrying most of the bags.

CLAUDIA: I thought this was a kvetch-free zone.
MARK: Well, now that you're shopping, it's no longer kvetch-free.
CLAUDIA: So you're paying, right?
MARK: I have Mario's credit card.

SANTIAGO DE COMPOSTELA

Santiago de Compostela has been the main event in Galicia for centuries because it is (reputedly) the site of the remains of Saint James the Apostle, Santiago. The remains were discovered in 835 by a shepherd, said to be guided to the location by a star (*compostela* means "field of stars"). The city's magnificent cathedral was started in 1075 under Alfonso VI but was not consecrated until 1128, under Alfonso IX. Santiago's significance in Catholic Europe is second only to that of Rome, and for centuries it has been the destination for millions of religious pilgrims who travel the Camino de Santiago, or the Way of Saint James, from the Pyrenees, or beyond, up to the church.

THE EMPANADA HUT

The almost-hidden empanada bakery looks like something from A Long Time Ago. It's a hut nestled in the middle of a forest, replete with thick fog, trees laden with apples and chestnuts, and blackberry bushes. We meet the bakers, who make everything look easy—which, for them, it is. They've done this a thousand times.

The dough consists only of flour, water, and salt—time replaces yeast. Once it's rolled out, the round of dough is placed on a piece of brown paper coated in olive oil. A mixture of chorizo, *panceta* (Spanish bacon), onions, and peppers is spread over the surface, and another round of dough is placed on top. The empanada makers work quickly and methodically. The end result is aromatic and satisfying.

EMPANADA

The name of this traditional savory pastry comes from the verb empanar, *which means to coat or cover with* pan *(bread).*

SERVES 6 TO 8

½ pound Spanish chorizo, casings removed and cut into ¼-inch dice

½ pound pancetta, cut into ¼-inch dice

1 large yellow onion, cut into ¼-inch dice

2 red bell peppers, cut into ¼-inch dice

2 pounds pizza dough (frozen is fine)

Olive oil

Cook the chorizo and pancetta in a large skillet over medium heat until they begin to render their fat, 5 to 8 minutes. Add the onion and peppers and cook until the chorizo and pancetta are well browned and the vegetables are softened, 9 to 12 minutes. Remove from the heat.

Cut the dough in half. Roll one piece out into a thin (¼ to ⅛ inch) round. Line a baking sheet with parchment and rub the paper with olive oil. Place the dough on the parchment and spread generously with olive oil. Spread the chorizo mixture evenly over the dough, leaving a ½-inch border all around. Roll out the second piece of dough. Moisten the exposed edges of the bottom round of dough with water, place the second round over the filling, and crimp the edges together with a fork to seal. Brush the dough liberally with olive oil and cut a few steam vents in the center. Bake in a 450°F oven for 25 to 30 minutes, or until the crust is golden. Serve hot or at room temperature.

MARIO: Sorry, Bitty, but while you were sleeping, they said the one that sleeps is the one who does all of the dishes and eats last.

MARK: What I thought you were going to say was that you are planning on eating this empananda all by yourself.

Men stand on the shores of the Miño with huge fishing poles and catch tiny fish—carp, *boga* (a ray-finned fish with a small head and a wide body), and small bass. On a good day, a fisherman can take home five hundred fish. The best way to prepare the fish, according to the man we talked to, is escabeche-style, basically marinating them in vinegar after cooking them.

MARIO: Wow, this place is smokin'. It's just so grand.

RECIPE

fisherman's
ESCABECHE

Escabeche is an age-old method for preserving fish; it's also a great way to impart flavor. We paid attention when one of the local fisherman described his particular recipe.

SERVES 4 TO 6

1 cup extra-virgin olive oil

Flour for dredging

Kosher salt and freshly ground
   black pepper

2 pounds small fish fillets—
   small oily fish such as
   sardines, mackerel, or
   bluefish work well

3 or 4 fresh bay leaves

12 garlic cloves, crushed
   and peeled

1 cup white vinegar

1 cup dry white wine

Heat ½ cup of the olive oil in a large skillet over medium heat until hot. Season the flour with salt and pepper. Working in batches, dredge the fish in the flour, shaking off the excess, add to the hot oil, and cook until golden brown, about 3 minutes per side. Transfer the fish to an earthenware casserole or baking dish that holds it snugly.

Clean the skillet, add the remaining ½ cup oil, and heat over medium heat until hot. Add the bay leaves and garlic and heat until fragrant, about 2 minutes. Add the vinegar and wine (be careful, the mixture will probably spit a bit) and bring just to a boil, then lower the heat and simmer for a few minutes to infuse the liquid. Pour over the fish and let cool to room temperature. Serve, or refrigerate for up to 3 days (serve at room temperature or slightly chilled).

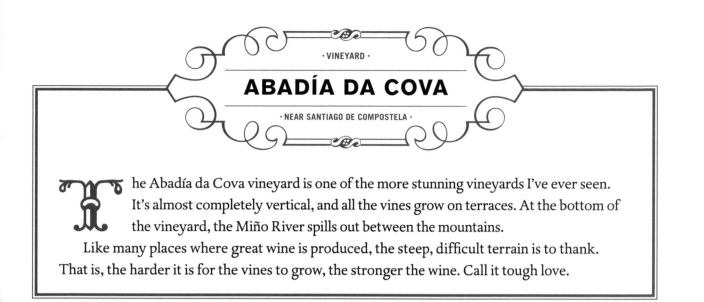

ABADÍA DA COVA

The Abadía da Cova vineyard is one of the more stunning vineyards I've ever seen. It's almost completely vertical, and all the vines grow on terraces. At the bottom of the vineyard, the Miño River spills out between the mountains.

Like many places where great wine is produced, the steep, difficult terrain is to thank. That is, the harder it is for the vines to grow, the stronger the wine. Call it tough love.

OCTOPUS
Galician-style

At the Abadía da Cova vineyard, the young pulpo (octopus) cook says that the only secret is experience—he knows when the octopus is done just by looking. He deftly cuts the tentacles into bite-sized pieces with scissors and dresses them with olive oil, salt, and pimentón.

SERVES 6 TO 8

One 6- to 8-pound octopus, cleaned and rinsed

Extra-virgin olive oil

Coarse sea salt

Hot pimentón (Spanish smoked paprika)

Bring a large pot of water to a boil. Add the octopus and bring back to a boil. Skim off the foam, reduce the heat to a gentle simmer, and cook for 5 minutes. Turn off the heat and let the octopus sit in the hot water for about an hour, or until tender.

Drain the octopus and cut into bite-sized pieces with kitchen shears. Toss with olive oil, salt, and pimentón to taste, and serve.

MARIO: Look at how beautiful this octopus is.

CLAUDIA: Yeah, I have seen a lot of cartoons and this reminds me of them.

MARIO: No tricks, no vegetables, no vinegar, just plain water and a little salt. Wow, this is the real deal.

RECIPE

QUEIMADA

Queimada is a traditional Galician punch made from potent orujo, sugar, lemon, and coffee. There's a ritual attached to it: first you recite a spell (we skipped that part), then you set it on fire. After all that, it turns out it's a pretty good drink, except it's very, very strong. Not that that's a bad thing.

SERVES 12

4 cups orujo

½ cup sugar

Peel of 1 lemon, cut into strips

¼ cup coffee beans

Put all the ingredients in an earthenware bowl. Say a spell or a prayer, if you wish. Using a long match, set the orujo on fire and stir for about 10 minutes, until the flames die down. Serve in small clay cups.

ORUJO: *Orujo*, sometimes called *aguardiente*, is a spirit native to Galicia with a very high alcohol level. It's a bit like Italian grappa or Peruvian pisco—it's made from the leftovers of the wine-making process, the grape skins and seeds, as well as bits of branches. Most people, excluding myself of course, can't drink a lot of it at once.

CLAUDIA'S THEORY on HOT DRINKS

Claudia believes that it's a myth that cold drinks cool you down in hot weather. She insists that when the sun is strong, you have to drink hot tea. I disagree, but she made a good point about my cheeks being rosier than hers. *Queimada*, the warm Galician punch, was the perfect drink to test her theory. I know it didn't cool me down, but that didn't stop me from having seconds.

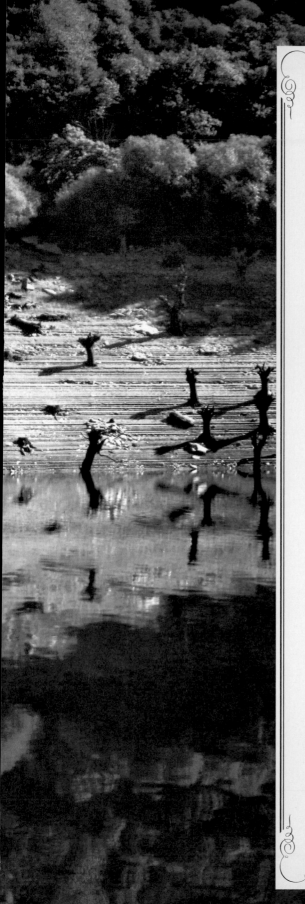

FAVORITE DRIVING MUSIC

GWYNETH:

I put the iPod on random and I get very excited if

ROXY MUSIC

SECRET MACHINES

INTERPOL, *or*

JUSTIN TIMBERLAKE *remixes come on.*

MARIO:

Everything from the

WHITE STRIPES

to **R.E.M.**

to **MOZART.**

CLAUDIA:

My "Top Ten" are

**THE CURE, THE 4 OF US, JOHNNY CASH,
NINA SIMONE, LOS ASLÁNDTICOS,
THE FRAMES, BRUCE SPRINGSTEEN, TEXAS,
BOB DYLAN,** *and* **ROBERT BRADLEY.**

MARK:

JAZZ

(but mostly I like to work or nap in the backseat).

WHAT WE'RE LOOKING FORWARD TO

We're on our way to Bilbao, east of Galicia but also on
Spain's northern coast, where we will meet Frank Gehry, eat
wonderful tapas, and spend time in wine country.

4

From BILBAO to ELCIEGO

We couldn't have picked a better time to be in Bilbao. It's the tenth anniversary of the Guggenheim Museum Bilbao and architect Frank Gehry is in town. After meeting him, we're inspired to drive to Elciego to visit the hotel he designed right in the vineyards that produce Marqués de Riscal wine.

Pintxos, Montaditos, Jamón, GRILLED VEGETABLES p. 118, borage

BASQUE COUNTRY

The Basque region, País Vasco, is more or less a country within a country. The area's nationalists have long sought independence from Spain and, despite the erratic, sometimes even dangerous, politics, Basque Country's self-contained attitude offers a certain warmth. It is an area at once enamored of tradition and intrigued by innovation; self-assured, País Vasco is able to invoke the new without losing the old. The three main cities—Bilbao, Vitoria, and San Sebastián—all demonstrate the adventurous confidence and curiosity of a twenty-first century urban center while maintaining the charm and character of a historical metropolis.

BILBAO

Diego López de Haro, a Vizcayan noble, founded Bilbao in 1300. Its location along the eastern end of the Camino de Santiago (see Chapter 2) led to its growth as a trade center, and its natural mineral wealth, combined with its position on the Nervion River, gave it unusual opportunity to benefit from the Industrial Revolution in the nineteenth century. Mining, steel production, and shipbuilding industries all contributed to Bilbao's growth, and by the beginning of the twentieth century, it was one of the richest cities in Spain. But politics inconsistent with Franco's left the city by the wayside, and by the end of Franco's rule, it was a postindustrial wasteland. Then boom: 1997. Everything changed in a year. Frank Gehry's masterpiece, the Guggenheim Museum, helped to establish Bilbao as a twenty-first century architectural and design destination. Yet with all of its newness, Bilbao has not lost its sense of history. El Casco Viejo, the Old Quarter, is still home to much of the city's cultural life, and against a backdrop of stone archways and long-established *pintxo* bars, urban hipsters bask in the city's rebirth.

PINTXOS

On any given evening, Bilbao's Plaza Nueva, built in 1821, echoes with children's laughter and grown-up chatter. The surrounding streets smell like garlic and are littered with napkins dropped by wandering partons of the many *pintxo* bars (*pintxo* is the Basque word for "tapa"). The best *montaditos*, a type of *pintxo*, are at Victor Montes, a *pintxo* bar in the plaza itself; here crab salad is piled high on slices of bread and topped with grated hard-boiled egg and caviar. The bartenders wear long striped aprons and use a knife and fork, held in one hand, to lift the *pintxos* from their platters onto small plates. Down the street from Victor Montes, Zuga is a modern joint specializing in bright colors and big flavors. *Chipirones*, baby squid, stained pink by the beet juice it cooked in, is served in a glass with a mint infusion. The best *jamón* seems to be over at Bukoi, where men with big bellies and slicked-back hair sing at the tables outside. The woman at the counter turns a hand-cranked slicer with a smooth mix of velocity and precision, and she rings bell when a plate is filled with the salty, silky king of pork.

¿QUÉ es?

KALIMOTXO: *Kalimotxo* is what teenagers drink all over Spain, but the tradition started in the Basque Country. Basically they mix equal parts of cheap red wine and Coca-Cola. This is one tradition I will never, ever, be down with.

MONTADITOS: A style of pintxo, a *montadito*—the name comes from the Spanish word for mountain—usually consists of a mayonnaise-bound salad mounded on rounds of bread.

MARK: Normally my theory is you pace yourself unless it's really good, and then you do what you have to do.

MARIO: Well, my thought has always been if something is this good, what could I possibly pace myself for? Something better? Not likely.

MARIO: Two words that I have always liked: "wrapped in ham."

MARK: Well, that's three words, but yes.

MARIO: That slicer is from 1904.

MARK: Older than both of us put together.

MARIO: The ink has the taste of the bottom of the sea; it's deep, murky, rich. And the calamari, cooked only for a minute, has the taste of the top of the sea, the foam. The smell, the salinity. God, I should write a book.

MARK: You make me want to quit my job—you're so much better at it.

GWYNETH: Where are Mario and Bittman?

CLAUDIA: They went to work out in the gym.

GWYNETH: Oh please, they're probably doing something illegal.

· MUSEUM ·
THE GUGGENHEIM
· BILBAO ·

Spanish novelist Manuel Vázquez Montalbán described the Museo Guggenheim Bilbao as a meteorite—an apt term considering the building's cultural impact, not to mention its out-of-this-world appearance. Gwyneth and I are fortunate to be able to meet with Gehry himself. When Gwyneth asks him how he's able to construct a structure like the Guggenheim, he replies that he "just does it." Gehry's response reflects his determined, fearless approach to architecture and design: for him, the impossible is merely a temptation.

GWYNETH and I TALK with FRANK GEHRY

GWYNETH: What happened to you that made you break with the traditional architecture and invent these unbelievable shapes?

GEHRY: I believe that there has to be a certain amount of passion in one's work. You have it in yours, I have it in mine.

GEHRY: Here there is a nineteenth-century city, there's the river, and then there's the bridge. What I liked about the city was the industrial toughness of it, which was saved by the green hills around it.

GWYNETH: Did you start with the external aspects of the building?

GEHRY: No, everyone thinks I do, but I don't. I'm a very traditional, functional worker.

MARIO: Was there ever a moment in the construction of this when you said, maybe my idea was too pure, or let's just make it easier? Or was that part of the challenge: it's going to get harder and harder, so let's just persevere.

GEHRY: No. The idea from the beginning was accepted by the clients.

GEHRY: The problem for me is how do you preserve the feelings, the passion, through the process of all of the people who are going to touch it, and that's what the miracle is of a building like this. Thousands of people's hands worked on this building, so how do I keep this energy? And that was something that I focused on from beginning to end.

GWYNETH: Why did you choose titanium for this building?

GEHRY: Bilbao has very few sunny days like today; it's pretty gray. I have been using metal on exteriors of buildings for a while. It's the only thing that you can make both a roof and a wall out of; I wanted to make three-dimensional things where the roof and the walls were the same. We made mock-ups of stainless steel, but it went dead, really dead, lifeless. I was very very frustrated about it. Then I found a piece of titanium in my office and nailed it to a telephone pole, and by some miracle it rained that day in Los Angeles, and the piece of titanium was golden, and I said, "Eureka!" That was the eureka moment.

We spent two years in the mills of the guys that make the titanium, that roll it. And it's like making the perfect salad. So it's a bit of oil and acid on the rollers. And after many, many iterations we got it like this. I have not been able to get it again, and I've tried. So this is really one of a kind. I know people using titanium, and they're not getting the character that this has.

GWYNETH: It's amazing, it's really has a depth to it that's incredible.

GEHRY: When it rains, it goes golden.

GWYNETH: It almost looks lit from within.

GEHRY: I think if you had a garage filled with old cars and junk and you had a Picasso and you lit it right, it would look great.

GEHRY: Coming here, it's like coming home.

GWYNETH: There is a tangible effect on people.

GEHRY: I think it's human nature to want to be part of something.

MARK *and* GEHRY HAVE LUNCH TOGETHER

MARK: Are you happy with all of this? This museum put Bilbao on the map.

GEHRY: The city planners knew that they had a generally depressed area that they had to refurbish. They had decided that culture was the catalyst for future.

From a financial point of view, the wild card, my building, was the conservative choice of the three choices. So it turned the word "conservative" on its head.

GEHRY: I work hard to make it look like it's immediate, that there is immmediacy, but it is all carefully contrived to be that.

MARK: Do you think that there is something in the Basque character that allowed people to see that the building would work in this space?

GEHRY: Well, they asked me for the Sydney Opera House so that was liberating but also scary because it's a kind of heavy request. But the Basque are a very straightforward people. The budget was $100 million, and there wasn't to be a cent more or a cent less spent.

When we first showed them the models, they were nervous about it, but they stayed the course.

MARK: There was a period in the 1980s and 1990s in New York where food was described as architectural, but all that really meant was that it was very tall.

GEHRY: I think that chefs today think visually. They are inspired by art, they do look at paintings, so it's normal for them to compose dishes.

I think the diet craze has made things prettier. Because they made things smaller.

MARK: They are much more composed. When you think about it, there's nothing weirder that you can put on a table than a whole roast turkey.

MARK: Were you big on building blocks when you were a kid?

GEHRY: I was. We were a rather poor family, so I didn't have much, but we used to get wood shavings from the local wood shop and my grandmother used to sit on the floor with me and fantasize cities. That's what came back to me when I thought about what I wanted to become. That was interesting because there was a middle-aged woman, sitting on the floor, suggesting that play could be done as an adult. A license to play as an adult, which I've kept in my mind all these years.

MARK: Do you think of this work as play?

GEHRY: In a sense it is, childlike.

GEHRY: The general public thinks I did the outside and then just jammed everything in, which is a fantastic misconception. It does come from the inside out: otherwise it doesn't work.

lciego, about an hour from Bilbao, is a small rural village in the Rioja region, home to the Marqués de Riscal vineyard since the mid-1850s. It is now also the site of Frank Gehry's new hotel and wine center, built in 2006 on the vineyard's grounds. With the wine in mind, Gehry chose shades of purple, white, and gold for his undulating metal exterior. The purple is said to represent the wine, the white the label, and the gold the famous Marqués de Riscal wire mesh that wraps itself around the bottle. There is a spectacular spa where vinous treatments are offered and wine therapy is practiced (I took a swim in the spa's pool at 2 a.m.; don't tell).

We taste two phenomenal wines at Marqués de Riscal. The first is the 2001 Reserva Baron de Chirel. Predominantly Tempranillo, it is rich, unusually lightly tannic, and soft enough for early drinking (just five years into the vintage). Slightly smoky and spicy, it is fruity and has a clear fungal undertone, with hints of cinnamon and cooked berries, and a luscious velvet finish.

We drink the second wine the following morning. We are in the Marqués de Riscal's barrel-lined caves, and the vineyard's director, Francisco Hurtado de Amézaga, opens a bottle of a 1958 wine taken from a dusty room filled floor to ceiling with old bottles. It's another world altogether. There is still very bright acidity in this mahogany package, with a sweet vanilla fragrance and tones of ripe plums in astonishing balance with its burgundian, mysterious juiciness. Truly a world-class wine with lots of time ahead of it—if I lived here, I would drink it all just because I could. A sublime wine experience at 9:55 a.m.

GWYNETH & CLAUDIA at the SPA

GWYNETH: I love how there is this spa in the middle of the vineyard, so you just finish and then you get bombed on red wine. It's detox to retox.

CLAUDIA: Yeah, first you swim in it and then you drink it.

DUELING BREAKFASTS

GWYNETH: yogurt with honey on the side, fruit, coffee with soymilk

MARIO: torta del Casar cheese, tongue terrine, eggs, sausage, thickly sliced rye bread with olive oil and crushed tomatoes, melon, espresso with sugar

GRILLED VEGETABLES

After I left the vineyard to go home to visit my family, Gwyneth and Mark met up with a local chef named Nino. He arranged for a wonderful lunch consisting of vegetables fresh from the lush Basque landscape. He put a metal grate on the ground, piled grapevines on top, and set them on fire. When the vines burned down, he threw some salt on the fire "to give it a little life," then grilled endive, carrots, leeks, eggplant, onions, and peppers. He served the grilled vegetables with boiled potatoes and borage, all doused with coarse salt and olive oil.

MARQUÉS DE RISCAL VINEYARD

Mario and Gwyneth eat grapes off the vine.

MARIO: You have to eat the pits too.

GWYNETH: Why?

MARIO: They tell you all about the wine. Come on, it's not that bad.

GWYNETH: It's not that great.

 ¿QUÉ es? **BORAGE**: When they brought the mystery vegetable out, my first reaction was that I wasn't eating it raw until someone told me I could. But then I realized it was, in fact, borage—a vegetable I used to grow in my garden. Borage, a bristly plant, can grow to be two or three feet high. It produces small blue flowers and also a lot of seeds; a plentiful plant, it tends to spread its way through the garden. It tastes like a cross between cucumber and celery. In northern Spain, it is traditionally boiled with potatoes and dressed with salt and olive oil. — **MARK**

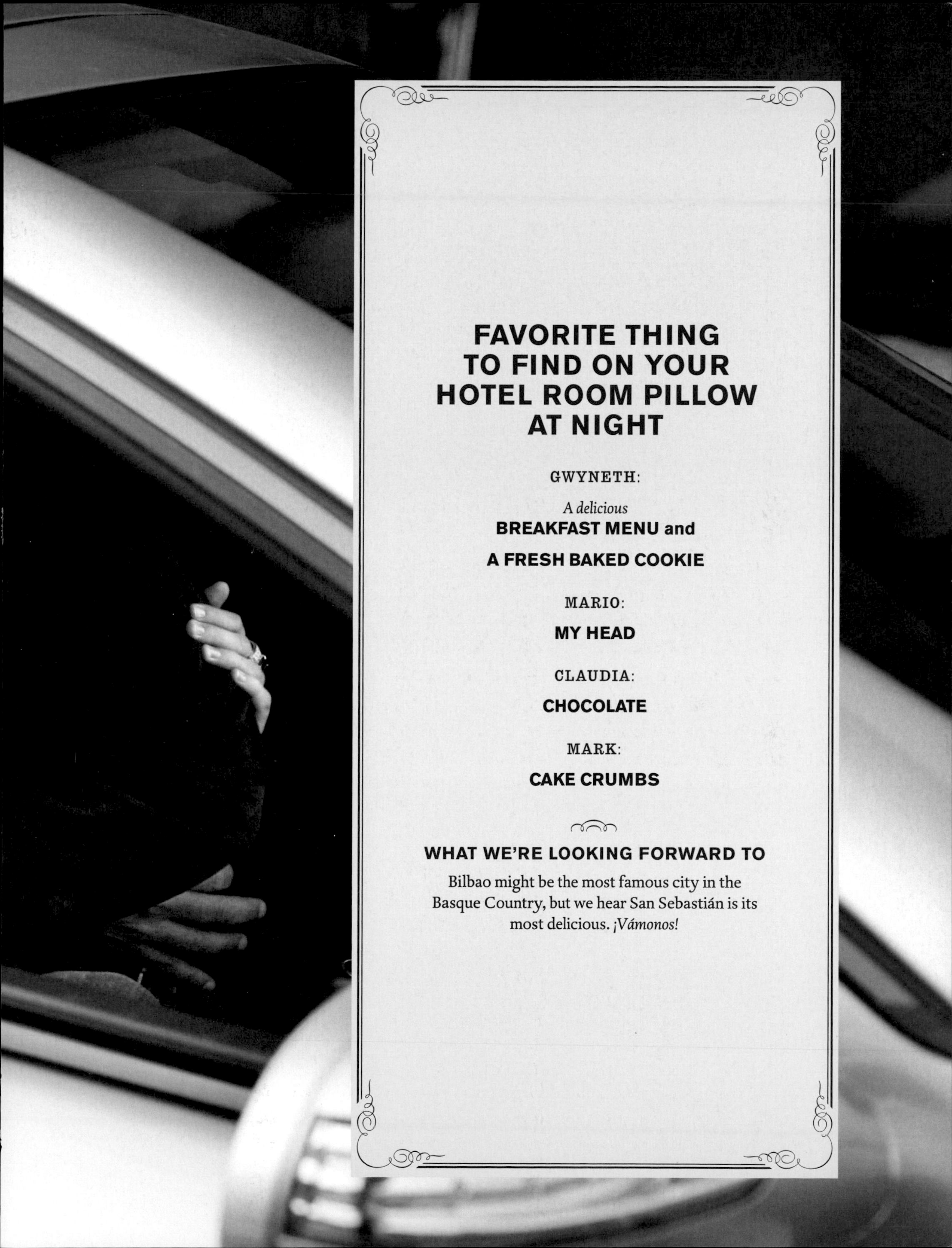

FAVORITE THING TO FIND ON YOUR HOTEL ROOM PILLOW AT NIGHT

GWYNETH:

A delicious
BREAKFAST MENU and

A FRESH BAKED COOKIE

MARIO:

MY HEAD

CLAUDIA:

CHOCOLATE

MARK:

CAKE CRUMBS

WHAT WE'RE LOOKING FORWARD TO

Bilbao might be the most famous city in the
Basque Country, but we hear San Sebastián is its
most delicious. *¡Vámonos!*

5

From VITORIA to SAN SEBASTIÁN

WHERE WE'RE GOING

I go to New York to spend some quality time with my family while Claudia and Mark make their way to San Sebastián via the ancient city of Vitoria, where they find a fascinating cathedral and excellent, smart tapas. They learn the ins and outs of Idiazabal cheese and spend time in San Sebastián with the nearly indescribable chef and restaurateur Juan Mari Arzak.

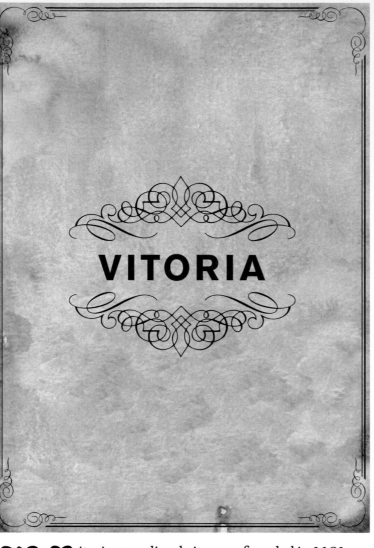

VITORIA

Vitoria, a medieval city, was founded in 1181 by Sancho el Sabio (the Wise). It is the Basque Country's capital and the second largest city after Bilbao. Claudia had never been there, but she told me that between the incredible cathedral and the restaurant Asador Sagartoki, she'll be back for sure.

Built in the thirteenth century, the Catedral de Santa María was shut down in 1994 for safety reasons. After six years of planning, reconstruction began in 2000 and is scheduled to end in 2014, but you can go in now. Entering the cathedral halfway through its transformation is a surreal experience replete with zigzagging catwalks, unearthed skeletons, and recently unveiled ancient city walls. It feels like stepping into two periods—then and now.

ASADOR SAGARTOKI

PINTXO MORUNO Y
PURE D HORTALIZAS

The bathrooms at Asador Sagartoki feature androgynous drawings of human beings—one says *"Soy un chico"* ("I'm a boy"), the other *"Soy una chica"* ("I'm a girl"). This kind of cleverness prevails throughout the restaurant, and the food has won many awards. Senén González, the young chef, has a charismatic smile and a lot of enthusiasm. His *pintxos* are presented in acrylic boxes on top of pedestals. Museum-quality specimens, the playful *pintxos* elevate traditional dishes to haute-cuisine status. Senén does not, however, abandon tradition—his floor, like that of any *pintxo* bar, is strewn with napkins.

FRIED EGGS

with potatoes (a conceptual dish)

Senén created this dish, based on the traditional Spanish combination of fried potatoes and eggs, as a "bite-sized memory." He has won awards specifically for this pintxo, *and he says that it has caused him a trauma, because since he invented it, "he hasn't been able to do something better."*

SERVES 12

FOR THE "POTATO PAPER"

1 pound baking potatoes, peeled
Kosher salt
Freshly grated nutmeg

TO FINISH

24 slices bacon, chilled
12 small eggs
Olive oil for shallow-frying

For the "potato paper," cook the potatoes in boiling salted water until tender. Drain and pass through a ricer or a food mill into a bowl. Add salt and nutmeg to taste. With a rubber spatula, spread the puree into a very thin layer on a 16-by-12-inch baking sheet lined with a silicone mat. Dry in a 170°F oven for 4 hours.

To assemble the tapas, lightly moisten the sheet of dried potatoes with a spray of water. Let stand for a minute, then remove the sheet from the pan and cut into 4-inch squares. Lay one slice of bacon across a second one to make a cross. Carefully crack one of the eggs, discard the white (or save for another use), and put the yolk in the center of the bacon cross. Carefully wrap the bacon around the egg yolk, overlapping the ends slightly, then trim as necessary to make a neat package without excess bacon. Repeat with the remaining bacon and egg yolks. Place each bacon parcel on a square of potato paper and wrap into a neat parcel.

In a large skillet, heat ½ inch of olive oil to 370°F. Working in batches, put the parcels seam side down in the oil and cook until the first side is golden and crisp, about 2 minutes. Turn the packages and cook until the other side is golden, about 2 minutes. Drain on paper towels and let cool slightly, then place on a platter. Warn your guests to eat their packets in a single bite, or their Hermés ties will be ruined.

Some of the best Idiazabal, a nutty-tasting cheese made from the milk of Latxa sheep, comes from the Idiazabal Village, which is just that—a village. It seems everyone who works there is related either by blood or by interest. They all wear traditional outfits, smile a lot, and call, *"¡Poliki! Poliki!"* to the sheep and dogs. *Poliki* translates, more or less, as "go peacefully." It's all very quaint but not at all hokey.

The driveway to the main building and the surrounding fields are overgrown with mint, parsley, wild onions, and greens. Sheep amble around, munching, and their diet gives their milk a subtly herbaceous quality. The village is a self-sufficient community, and its gardens overflow with Swiss chard, kale, lettuces, tomatoes, pepper, potatoes, leeks, and zucchini with big orange blossoms. At lunchtime, Mark and Claudia sit down at a wooden table covered with platters of tomatoes, spicy roasted peppers, bread, walnuts, apple wine, and, of course, Idiazabal.

CHEESE CHITCHAT

CLAUDIA: The cheese will warm up slowly; the process is very slow.

MARK: Patience, patience, patience, Claudia. I love how making this cheese has to be done a little bit by hand, that there are a lot of judgment calls. It's not just turn on the machine and walk away, it's an art.

SAN SEBASTIÁN

Colorful boats, white bridges, and kitschy lampposts mark San Sebastián, a seaside city on the northern coast that looks as if it belongs among Spain's southern beach towns. A relaxed atmosphere reigns—in fact, San Sebastián was traditionally the summer residence of Spanish royalty. The city's main industry, aside from tourism, harks back to its history as a fishing village. San Sebastián was given political status in 1174 only because its bay allowed the kingdom of Navarra access to whale and cod. Speaking of fish, San Sebastián is probably the best eating city in the Basque Country, which is one of the best eating regions in the country.

JUAN MARI ARZAK

Juan Mari Arzak may be more famous in San Sebastián than the mayor. A short, stout man of sixty-five, he has a warm spirit and a hearty laugh. Sporting hip eyeglasses, he travels via scooter, and he promises to start a diet every day—well, every tomorrow.

Juan Mari and his daughter, Elena, are responsible for putting San Sebastián on the culinary map. His eponymous restaurant, housed in a building constructed in 1897 by his grandparents, has three deserved Michelin stars. His modern, high-design food is based on traditional dishes from the area, the food he grew up eating. But he makes a point of distinguishing roots from tradition—the latter, he argues, is a construct. "You have to know your roots," Juan Mari says, "or else you've got nothing."

ON THE FISHING BOAT WITH JUAN MARI

MARK: Did you see these bait fish? They look like dinner to me.

CLAUDIA: What are they?

MARK: I think they're sardines. He just picked one up! He just put his hand in and grabbed it! Let's try!

CLAUDIA: I don't like seeing them agonized.

TAPAS *with* **JUAN MARI**

There's a strong *pintxo* tradition in San Sebastián, and no one appreciates "going *tapeo*" quite like Juan Mari. Before the drinks are poured, he has already put back two or three *montaditos* (a piece of bread mounded with a mayonnaise-based salad), not to mention nearly an entire platter of *jamón*.

Juan Mari finds freedom in *pintxos*: "You have different foods, wines—there are possibilities. You stand up, you are very free. It's popular, everyone eats *pinxtos*. You move, it's fast. It's one moment and then another." He is everywhere at once, all of the time.

At La Cepa, our first stop, the tables display curiosity collections under glass (seashells, game pieces, etc.) and the bartenders pour *clarete* (basically rosé from Ribera del Duero) freely. There's a beer tap shaped like a leg of *jamón*. Rounds of bread are draped with *boquerones* (little anchovies in vinegar) or salt-preserved anchovies, small boiled eggs are wrapped in *jamón* with a shrimp and olive skewered on top. The most addictive *pintxos* are the *pimientos de Gernika* with anchovies and olives threaded onto toothpicks. The peppers are small and thin, and you eat the whole skewered affair in one messy, vinegary bite.

At Ganbara, our next stop, the entire bar is covered in *pintxo* platters—there's nowhere to put a glass, save an elbow. The foot-high piles of mushrooms are not just for show—here an order of *hongos con huevo* rewards you with a plate of different mushrooms, all perfectly cooked, with a raw egg yolk in the middle. The egg mixes with the mushroom juices and the bit of olive oil left from the sauté pan—a silky, mushroomy wonder.

¿QUÉ **¿es?** **PIMIENTOS DE GERNIKA**: *Pimientos de Gernika* are short, thin, not-too-spicy peppers from the Basque town of Gernika (Guernica). In 1937, during the Spanish Civil War, the Nazis bombed Gernika on Franco's orders, killing hundreds of civilians and destroying the town. Picasso's famous *Guernica*, now housed in Madrid's Reina Sofía Museum, commemorates the tragic occasion.

MUSHROOMS
with egg yolk

This is one of the easiest ways to prepare mushrooms, but it is also decadent and impressive. The Basque Country is known for its mushrooms, and you find this dish in pintxos bars all around the region.

SERVES 4

¼ cup plus 1 tablespoon extra-virgin olive oil

1 pound porcini or mixed wild mushrooms, cut into ⅛-inch-thick slices

1 garlic clove, minced

4 large eggs

2 tablespoons finely chopped Italian parsley

Kosher salt and freshly ground black pepper

Heat ¼ cup of the oil in a large skillet over medium-high heat. Add the mushrooms and sauté for about 5 minutes, or until beginning to soften. Add the garlic and cook for 3 to 5 minutes, or until the mushrooms are nicely browned and softened. Remove from the heat and cover to keep warm.

Fry the eggs sunny-side up in the remaining 1 tablespoon oil in a large nonstick skillet until the whites are set but the yolks are still runny. Transfer to a cutting board and cut away the whites from the yolks (discard the whites). Spoon the mushrooms onto four plates and sprinkle with the parsley, salt, and pepper. Make a little space in the center of each portion of mushrooms, and nestle the yolks in the mushrooms. As you eat, mix the yolk with the hot mushrooms to create a rich, silky sauce.

IN THE KITCHEN *with* JUAN MARI

Juan Mari's kitchen is big, bright, impeccably clean—
and reeks of success. He shows Claudia how to make
his favorite fish, hake, which he eats every day.

 BANDERILLA: *Banderilla* refers to a *pintxo*
consisting of a pickled pepper, anchovy, and
olive skewered on a toothpick. *Banderilla* is
also the word for the sharp spears bullfight-
ers use; it comes from *bandera*, the word for flag, because
the bullfighters' painted spears are as colorful as flags.

HAKE
with clams and parsley

Claudia had never made hake before and now this recipe, which Mark says is the most useful one in the book, is in her repertoire.

SERVES 4

3 tablespoons olive oil

2 tablespoons finely chopped Italian parsley

1 teaspoon finely minced garlic

Four 6-ounce hake fillets (or substitute cod or haddock), skin on

1 tablespoon all-purpose flour

10 Manila or other small clams, scrubbed

Combine the olive oil, half the parsley, and the garlic in a cazuela or sauté pan large enough to hold the fish and clams in a single layer. Sprinkle the hake on both sides with salt and add to the cazuela, skin side down. Dust the fish with flour, then add the clams and ½ cup water and bring to a simmer. Cook for 2 minutes, then turn the fish, lower the heat, and simmer very gently until the clams open and the fish is cooked through, about 5 minutes. Divide the fish and clams among four plates, stir the pan juices, and spoon over the fish and into the clams. Sprinkle with the remaining parsley and serve.

COCOCHAS
al pil-pil

This is perhaps the most Basque of all Basque dishes. Hake contains a tremendous amount of natural gelatin (collagen) and, when prepared in this way, the gelatin emulsifies with the olive oil to create a wonderful loose quasi-mayonnaise. Since it might be hard to find hake cheeks, not to mention the special clay pot with a separate handle that Juan Mari uses, you can substitute cod cheeks or hake fillet for the cocochas and a sauté pan for the cazuela.

SERVES 3 TO 4

About 18 cocochas (hake or cod
    cheeks; you can substitute
    8-ounce hake fillet, cut into
    1-inch pieces)
½ teaspoon sea salt
2 tablespoons finely minced
    Italian parsley,
      plus extra for garnish
1 teaspoon finely minced garlic
Good olive oil

Arrange the cocochas in a single layer in a cazuela that holds them snugly. Sprinkle with the salt, parsley, and garlic, and add enough olive oil to come halfway up the cocochas. Bring to a simmer over medium heat, then reduce the heat and cook at a bare simmer for about 10 minutes, until the cheeks are just cooked through.

Pour off the oil and reserve. Attach a handle to the cazuela, and add a few drops of room-temperature water and a bit of the reserved olive oil, swirling the dish to mix. Continue adding the olive oil little by little and swirling the dish rapidly until the sauce is emulsified and thick and coats the cocochas, about 5 minutes; if necessary, add a bit of water to keep the mixture under 200°F. Sprinkle with parsley and serve.

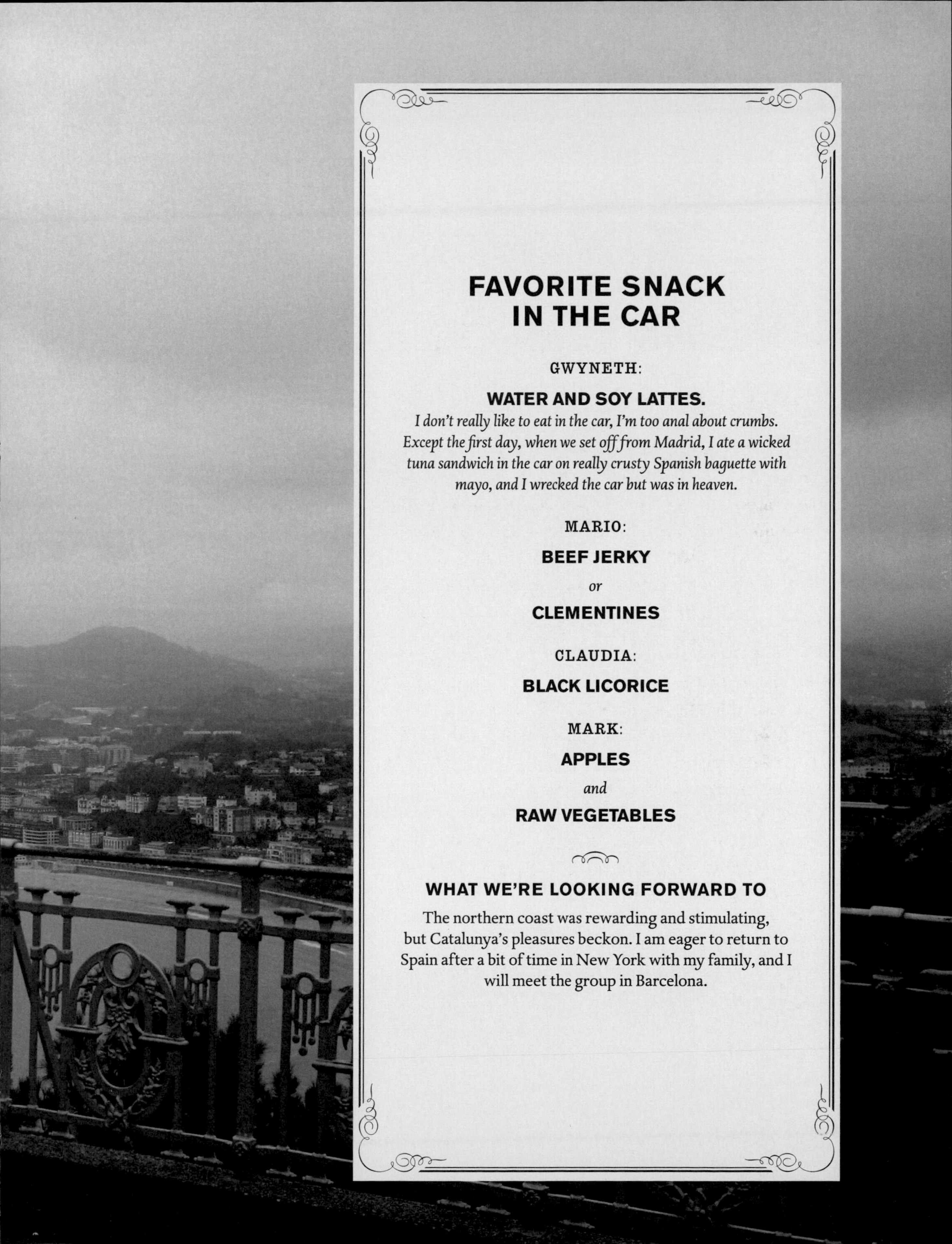

FAVORITE SNACK IN THE CAR

GWYNETH:

WATER AND SOY LATTES.
*I don't really like to eat in the car, I'm too anal about crumbs.
Except the first day, when we set off from Madrid, I ate a wicked
tuna sandwich in the car on really crusty Spanish baguette with
mayo, and I wrecked the car but was in heaven.*

MARIO:

BEEF JERKY

or

CLEMENTINES

CLAUDIA:

BLACK LICORICE

MARK:

APPLES

and

RAW VEGETABLES

WHAT WE'RE LOOKING FORWARD TO

The northern coast was rewarding and stimulating,
but Catalunya's pleasures beckon. I am eager to return to
Spain after a bit of time in New York with my family, and I
will meet the group in Barcelona.

6

From BARCELONA to GIRONA

CATALUNYA

Catalunya sits in the northeastern corner of Spain, and it's got a lot to be proud of: the region boasts wonderful architecture (Gaudí!), art (Picasso! Miró! Dalí!), and food (Ferran Adrià!). Barcelona, the capital, is about two thousand years old, but its embrace of contemporary design, fashion, and music makes it feel young and inventive. This youthful feel can be attributed to the post-Franco atmosphere—in 1975, after he died, the Catalan language came back into popularity and the city's businesses experienced new freedom and successes. Catalunya's varied history is also endowed with a fresh attitude and intrepid creativity.

Long considered by Madrileños as the second city of Spain, Barcelona, Catalunya's first city, is said to have been founded four centuries before Rome by Hercules. It was rebuilt in the third century BC, sometime after the first Punic War, by famed Carthaginian Barcas, who gave the city his family name. The Roman army used the town as a camp from late in the first century BC until it was sacked by the Visigoths in the fifth century. Taken over by the Moors in the eighth century, it was transformed by the family of Charlemagne, son Louis specifically, and it thrived until Aragon and Catalonia were loosely united by Barcelonan Count Berenguer's wedding to Petronila of Aragon. Catalonia's willingness to back the Hapsburgs in the War of Spanish Succession led to its loss of influence in Bourbon-ruled Spain, and Barcelona was really in a slippery spot politically until its power as a textile and machinery center emerged in the mid-nineteenth century. Gaudí and Dalí put their imprint on the cultural identity of the city, and Barcelona has been a serious contender for first city of Spain since the middle of the twentieth century (despite Franco's disdain).

ts Mediterranean weather makes Barcelona a very walkable city all year round. There is nothing like walking the Ramblas (Barcelona's main boulevard), always filled with life, artists, flowers, even animals. Then just make a detour onto any of the many tiny, beautiful little streets in the Gothic Quarter and discover your own personal vision of Barcelona.

Barcelona is full of art anywhere you go. Examples of modernist architecture are scattered all over the city, beautifully integrated, a magical halo composing the skyline. It's almost as if you were in a fairy tale: you can feel the presence of the great modernists, Gaudí, Puig i Cadafalch, Domènech i Montaner, conversing through their art in a timeless dance.

And then there is the sea. I have become so used to it, to seeing it, to smelling it, that I can never be too long anywhere where there is no sea, I feel claustrophobic without it. One of the things I love to do in Barcelona is to go to a *chiringuito* (snack bar) on the beach and eat some seafood and paella, then go for a walk along the shore. This recharges my batteries like nothing else. —CLAUDIA

THE STIPE SETUP

I arranged for Michael Stipe, Gwyneth's and my very good friend, to meet us in Catalunya. I kept it a secret, and when he arrived, I asked him to stand on the side of the road we'd be traveling and pretend to be a hitchhiker. Needless to say, Gwyneth was completely surprised.

MARIO: We could drive in this secluded area for 200 miles and not see a single soul.

GWYNETH: Except for this random dude inexplicably standing in the road.

MARIO: Inexplicably hitchhiking on our secluded road.

GWYNETH: Oh, my god! Oh, my god!

· RESTAURANT ·

INOPIA

· BARCELONA ·

Quick sketches, in a quasi-Basquiat style, of skewered food, champagne glasses, saltshakers, and other *cosas de tapas* (tapas things) cover the walls and columns at Inopia. The staff wears black T-shirts that have patches on the sleeves and the back, kind of NASCAR-driver style and they toss packs of cigarettes back and forth. The bathrooms have bar codes printed on the walls, and there are bottles of homemade pimentón-and-vinegar sauce at nearly every other stool. It's hip, to say the least.

But it's also sophisticated, thoughtful, and fanatically energetic. Run by Alberto Adrià, brother of famed Ferran, Inopia serves traditional Catalan tapas—precise ingredients cooked simply, if at all. A long ceramic dish of olives—delicious little malagueñas— is brought out first. Then a *boda* (literally, a wedding) of anchovies, both salt-cured and vinegar-cured. *Pan con tomate*, of course. Then icy-cold bacalao on crunchy bread (*pan de aire*, which translates as "bread of air") with olive paste. Next, perfect wedges of green but sweet tomato with tuna belly and scallions. And then *jamón*, seared tuna, fried *gambas* (shrimp), tiny fried mullets ("this is my favorite, because I have to work," says Michael), and anchovies infused with lemon, dredged in flour, and fried. Gwyneth says she's full and I tell her she's only started to see the edge of full. We're not done yet, not even close. Out come baby cuttlefish cooked *a la plancha*; *croquetas de jamón* made with Ibérico ham; eggplant with cane sugar; *patatas bravas* (fried potatoes with spicy tomato sauce and allioli, Gwyneth's absolute favorite); spiced lamb brochettes; torta Cañarejal cheese; pineapple with lime zest and molasses; strawberries with black pepper and sherry vinegar caramel; and finally, small glasses of homemade red peach wine. Michael perfectly renames it: "I'm going to call this place Utopia."

PINEAPPLE
with lime and molasses

This was a great dish to end the meal—a little sweet, a little acidic, it's a wonderfully flavorful, unexpected combination. Michael's father, who lives in Georgia, loves pineapple and, being a Southern man, loves molasses, so Michael purchased a jar of Inopia's molasses to bring back home. Alberto couldn't believe that Michael was going to carry the jar around Europe, but he eventually got it back home.

SERVES 8

1 ripe pineapple, peeled, cored, and cut into bite-sized pieces

Grated zest of 1 lime

3 tablespoons robust molasses

Put the pineapple on a plate, sprinkle it with the zest, and drizzle with the molasses. Enjoy.

MALAGUEÑAS: They serve the most amazing olives at Inopia. Gwyneth's favorite were the little malagueñas. The word *malagueña* is also the name of a traditional flamenco dance from Málaga, but the countryside around Málaga, in southern Spain, is covered in olive groves. **PACHARAN**: *Pacharan* is a Spanish after-dinner drink that's a bit like sloe gin. It's made from sloe berries and anise seeds and sometimes other flavorings as well—coffee beans, lemon peel, and vanilla beans are common. They make their own at Inopia with red peaches, and Michael described it as "amazing plum urine."

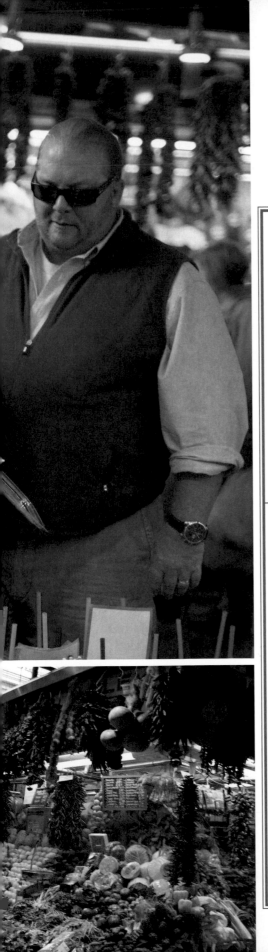

LA BOQUERÍA

La Boquería, also known as Mercat de Sant Josep, is Barcelona's famous market. It's located right off Las Ramblas and it's animated, colorful, and utterly absorbing. Michael, Claudia, and I go to the famous Bar Pinoxto, located inside the market, for *chipirones* (baby squid), *cafés con leche*, croissants *a la plancha*, and chickpeas with mushrooms. Claudia has to stop at the candy store, and we all enjoy watching the fishmongers and the *jamón* guys. A great morning!

CLAUDIA: He won't tell me what's in it, he says we just have to try it.

MICHAEL: For you, I will try anything.

MARIO: Ahh, first thing in the morning, there is nothing better than a little squid, a little coffee, and a little beer.

MICHAEL: Why are these chickpeas so delicious?

MARIO: Because it's October. They have just harvested them, so they have never been dried—they're fresh.

MICHAEL: I am a terrible cook, but I love to eat.

CLAUDIA: So we need Mario then.

LA CLARA

laudia and I head over to a modern restaurant, La Clara, that serves great tapas. We try a bunch of dishes, the most memorable being the fried brains. It's the first time Claudia's tried them and her response is pretty incredible: "Eating brains, I have to say, has a lot to do with psychology." The large poster of food in the restaurant, shown in the photo below, is actually a map of Barcelona—the asparagus, for example, represents the Sagrada Familia.

¿QUÉ es? **UNA CLARA**: The restaurant La Clara reminded me of a funny drink, *una clara*. Half beer, half fizzy lemon soda. It's what the girls drink.

Gwyneth is a spokeswoman for Estée Lauder and she was scheduled to make an appearance at the El Corte Inglés department store. They took photos and she gave autographs, then she quickly decamped to the store's supermarket with Claudia to buy snacks for the road.

WHILE DRIVING, A MAN TRIES TO PICK UP GWYNETH AND CLAUDIA

CLAUDIA: He is asking us who we are.

GWYNETH: We're nobody.

CLAUDIA: This is Carla and I'm Ana.

CLAUDIA: That man just said that he would marry you.

GWYNETH: Well, that's nice of him.

SANT PAU

A seaside town just barely an hour north of Barcelona, Sant Pol de Mar sits on the Costa de Barcelona-Maresme. Rocky and still a bit untamed, the coast has managed to avoid big real-estate developments. Its towns are small, long established, and unpretentious.

RESTAURANTE SANT PAU

The ideology behind Carme Ruscalleda's cooking is infectious. I am totally into her. She is a three-star Michelin chef who worked as a sandwich lady and raised her own pigs before opening her restaurant. She is attentive and devoted, alert and articulate.

Her kitchen is a cook's dream—a large Thirode stove, bigger than a billiards table, sits in the center, and a room-long window looks out at the garden and the ocean beyond. Her food is seasonal and local—and it takes a team of twenty-two chefs to make it (they serve only thirty-five customers at a time). The carefully constructed dishes require entire mornings of such tasks as peeling roasted pearl onions, filling tiny silicone molds with olive oil and raisins, and measuring the diameter of soupspoons to plan presentations.

Carme taught Gwyneth and me to make two fish dishes, and then she kicked us out of the kitchen to prepare a lunch that blew my mind.

GWYNETH: Carme has been cooking ever since she was little. Her family got their milk directly from the cow, and basically got everything directly from nature. She grew up watching the transformation of the raw ingredient, milk, to ice cream or cheese.

FISH
cooked in fig leaves

Carme prepared this dish simply, but with incredible thought. She used one element, figs, in three ways: fruit, leaf, and jam. This is really a recipe that one assembles more than cooks.

SERVES 1

2 organic fig leaves, washed

Kosher salt

One 5- to 6-ounce white fish fillets (hake is good)

1 ripe fresh fig, stemmed, thin skin removed, and quartered

1 small leek, white part only, halved lengthwise, and rinsed well

About 2 tablespoons olive oil

A few drops of dry vermouth

1 tablespoon fig jam

1 thick slice hazelnut or other brioche, toasted and broken into small croutons

Place 1 of the fig leaves in a small baking dish, underside facing up; set aside. Lightly salt the fish, fig, and leek and drizzle with the oil. Heat a plancha or a skillet over high heat, add the fish, fig, and leek, and cook, turning once, until lightly browned on both sides. Transfer to the baking dish and sprinkle with a bit more olive oil and the vermouth. Fold the remaining fig leaf in half and attach to the piece of fish with a toothpick. Place the dish in a 375°F oven and cook for a few minutes, just until the fish is firm to the touch. Transfer to a plate and serve with the jam, croutons, and any juices remaining in the dish. The dish should look artful but not too forced—a small pile of jam, the fish leaning just so, the croutons, leek, and fig nicely distributed.

FRIED FISH
with curry sauce

Carme used small local fish for this preparation, and she left the scales on the fillets. When they were fried, the scales got supercrispy—almost like tiny potato chips. Although this recipe has several different components, the assembly is very simple, and the result sublime.

SERVES 2

4 to 6 cups extra-virgin olive oil, for deep-frying

Four 3-ounce white fish fillets, such as perch or cod, skin on

Kosher salt and freshly ground black pepper

Flour for dredging

6 spinach leaves

Curry Sauce (recipe follows)

1 tablespoon toasted pine nuts

1 tablespoon toasted pistachios

I tablespoon dried currants

Heat 3 inches of olive oil in a medium heavy pot until it reaches 380°F. Sprinkle the fish with salt and pepper, dredge in the flour, shaking off the excess, and add to the hot oil. Fry for about 3 minutes, turning occasionally, until browned and crisp. Transfer to a plate. Add the spinach to the hot oil and fry for about 30 seconds, until bright green and crispy. Spoon the sauce over the fish and garnish with the spinach leaves, pine nuts, pistachios, and currants.

curry sauce   MAKES ABOUT 1 CUP

2 tablespoons olive oil

½ cup finely diced onion

½ cup finely diced carrot

½ cup finely diced apple

½ cup finely diced celery

1 tablespoon hot curry powder

1 teaspoon kosher salt

½ teaspoon freshly ground black pepper

2 tablespoons cold butter

Heat the olive oil in a large sauté pan over medium-high heat. Add the onion, carrot, apple, and celery and sauté for 5 to 8 minutes, or until beginning to soften. Add the curry powder, salt, and pepper and cook, stirring, for 5 minutes, or until the vegetables are soft. Add 1 cup water and bring to a boil, then lower the heat and simmer gently for 5 minutes. Transfer the mixture to a blender and puree until smooth, adding a bit more water if necessary. Pass through a fine-mesh sieve into a clean saucepan, set over low heat, and add the butter bit by bit, stirring just until it is incorporated. Serve.

SEGURA VIUDAS

ava, the Spanish sparkling wine, is named for the caves where it is aged. It's based in this kind of familiarity, rooted in this kind of tradition. At Segura Viudas, the corks are still put in by hand, and the bottles are manually rotated twice a day. It sounds charming, but it becomes a bit overwhelming if you have to apply the labor to the 20 million bottles they have at Segura Viudas.

The cava-making process involves two fermentations. The first is the usual wine fermentation in large barrels; the second occurs in the bottle, after the addition of sugar and yeast. Here the bottles are held in 25,000-square-meter caves. There are a few empty spaces in the cava grids—every now and then a bottle explodes. After they have fermented and aged, the bottles are put onto slanted stands that look kind of like sandwich boards, and the turning and rotating begins, in order to transport the sediment to the neck of the bottle. Then things get cool—very cool. The neck of each bottle is dipped into liquid nitrogen to freeze the sediment portion into an ice cube. The bottle is quickly opened, pressure forces the ice cube out, the bottle is topped off with a little more cava and a bit of sugar (this is called the dosage) and a fresh cork is plugged into place.

MARIO: The Spaniards make their cava for the people—I like a world based on sharing.

Gwyneth and I head over to the René Barbier vineyard and bodega. We plan to just drink wine, but they had a beautiful spread of ingredients, so we set up a grill on their roof and made lunch. It was especially surprising to find a large platter of *espardeñas* (sea cucumbers). Along with *gambas* and loads of fresh vegetables, they made a quick, satisfying lunch that was definitively Catalan.

MIXED GRILL
Catalan-style

You can grill just about anything. We were lucky to have some espardeñas (sea cucumbers) on our hands, so we mixed them with a few gambas (shrimp), peppers, and onions and had a wonderful lunch.

SERVES 4

12 large shrimp in the shell

1 pound espardeñas (sea cucumber), cleaned and soaked in cold water for 5 minutes (or substitute 1 pound large sea scallops)

2 red bell peppers, cut into wide strips

2 large onions, cut into ½-inch-thick rings

2 to 3 tablespoons olive oil

Coarse sea salt

Rub the shrimp, *espardeñas*, peppers, and onions with olive oil. Grill over a hot fire, turning once, until the seafood is cooked through and the vegetables are tender, about 2 to 3 minutes per side for the seafood and a few more minutes for the vegetables. Transfer to a platter, sprinkle with salt, and serve.

¿QUÉ es?

ESPARDEÑA: *Espardeña* is the Spanish word for "sea cucumber." It's also the Spanish word for "espadrille." Apparently, to the Spaniards' wild imagination, a sea cucumber looks like a shoe.

Anyhow, a sea cucumber is an echinoderm, meaning, like starfish, it has a hard spiny covering of skin. They look like slimy cucumbers made of leather. Appetizing? Not to hold in your hand, but they're actually quite tasty, especially when grilled. You usually buy them already cleaned, and they can simply be coated with olive oil, sprinkled with salt and pepper, and grilled for a couple of minutes on each side or, in my favorite style, cooked *a la plancha*. They're difficult to find fresh in the United States, but check your local Asian market.

PAN CON TOMATE

Perhaps the most emblematic of all Catalan food, pan con tomate (bread with tomato) is served everywhere with everything. It's more a method than a recipe. Gwyneth especially loves it when it's topped with a few boquerones (anchovies).

A few slices of Catalan or
    peasant bread
A garlic clove, halved
Extra-virgin olive oil
A really ripe tomato, cut in half
Coarse sea salt

Grill the bread or toast it under the broiler until browned on both sides. Rub with the garlic and drizzle with as much olive oil as you like. Rub and smash the tomato against the bread so that the pulp saturates the toast. Sprinkle with salt, and enjoy.

RECIPE

SPINACH Catalan-style

There's nothing like a nice plate of spinach. It just makes you feel good. The pine nuts and currants in this version lend texture and sweetness.

SERVES 2 TO 3

2 tablespoons olive oil
3 tablespoons pine nuts
3 tablespoons dried currants
1 large bunch spinach, washed
    and spun mostly dry (leave
    enough water to help cook
    the spinach)
Kosher salt and freshly ground
    black pepper

Heat the olive oil in a large skillet over medium-high heat (or over a hot grill fire). Add the nuts and currants and stir for a minute or two, until the nuts start to brown. Add the spinach, in batches if necessary, and stir and cook until the spinach is nicely wilted, 3 to 5 minutes. Season with salt and pepper, and serve.

GIRONA

A beautiful walled city with much to see, Girona was settled by the Ausetani people in the second century BC. The Romans built an outpost here that was later overtaken by the Visigoths, who in turn kept it until the arrival of the Moors. Charlemagne captured it in the late eighth century and made Girona one of the original Catalan countships. Alfonso I officially recognized it as a city in the mid-1060s, and it became a significant center of business and religion. The Catholic kings gave everyone but the Catholics the boot in the last decade of the fifteenth century, and the city survived sackings and attacks by various instruments of the French government up through the mid-nineteenth century.

In the interest of expansion, the city tragically destroyed much of the original walls, but over the last thirty years, Girona has spent much time and money repairing the walls. Now the Passeig de la Muralla makes an impressive tourist road around the older part of the town . . . love it! There are also amazing remains of the Jewish ghetto from the eighth to eleventh centuries. Today the whole well-restored area in the center of town is quite stunning.

JEWISH MUSEUM AND SYNAGOGUE

The old part of Girona is lined with medieval buildings, and walking the stone streets is like being thrown into the past. Especially interesting are the old synagogue and the Jewish Museum, which has Spain's biggest collection of Jewish tombstones: maybe a little bit morbid, but still and all a fascinating cultural assemblege.

MARIO: It's a pretty big little town.

GWYNETH: Indoor plumbing in the thirteenth century? Man, they really had it down.

FAVORITE ICE CREAM FLAVOR

GWYNETH:

JAMOCA ALMOND FUDGE
from Baskin-Robbins, but any artisanal
PUMPKIN
gelato will do.

MARIO:

OLIVE OIL
or
COFFEE.

CLAUDIA:

DULCE DE LECHE.

MARK:

I HAVE TO CHOOSE?

WHAT WE'RE LOOKING FORWARD TO

I am missing my family, so I'm headed to
New York for a bit. Gwyneth, Mark, and Claudia
will head off on the long drive south and enjoy
Andalucía without me. Ah!

7

From GRANADA to CÓRDOBA

WHERE WE'RE GOING

I still can't believe that I missed going to the Alhambra, but, then again, Halloween is one of the most important days of the year in the Batali family, so I had to be in New York City. Gwyneth and Mark tour the magnificent palace while Claudia sleeps in, but she manages to get there by the afternoon. Wonderful food, sort of half Spanish and half North African, is consumed, and then Córdoba calls for Mark and Claudia.

WHAT WE'RE EATING

BEET AND WALNUT PUREE p. 179, Pomegranates, FIDEOS WITH SEAFOOD p. 185, TEJERINGOS p. 187, FRIED EGGPLANT, p. 193, SALMOREJO p. 194, RABO DE TORO p. 195, FLAMENQUINES p. 196

GRANADA

When the Moors ruled Spain, Granada was the place to be. The Alhambra, the fortress and palace of Moorish kings, sits in the southeast district of the city and still stands, with all its old magnificence, as a reminder of times past. The city was named for the pomegranate, and Granada is just like the fruit—exotic and complicated. Originally settled by Iberian Celts, it was later occupied by the Phoenicians and then the Greeks. The Romans followed, and then the Visigoths, but Granada became the true center of Moorish culture on the Iberian Peninsula in the thirteenth century. Forced out of Córdoba and having given up Moorish Sevilla, offered as a trade, Mohamed ibn Alhamar Nasr, founder of the last and most elaborate Moorish dynasty, took over Granada in the late 1220s, and he built the Alhambra. In 1236, Granada was granted the exception of a vassal state to the Castile and the kingdom of Granada was allowed to continue under Arab rule until 1492, when Boabdil, "The Boy King," surrendered to the Catholic kings' intention to rid Spain of Arab and Jewish influence and went into exile. From then onward, each decade brought with it a little more Christian architecture, as Iberian Spaniards reestablished the town's Castilian rule and culture. Today Granada is one of the best places in Spain to experience the incredible and rich history of Moorish rule on the Iberian Peninsula.

Granada's proximity to Morocco, not to mention the historical influence of the Moors, has heavily influenced the city's cuisine. Falafel joints butt up against tapas bars, and mint tea is as plentiful as red wine.

At Rincón de la Aurora, one of Granada's best Arab restaurants, fattoush salad is heavy on the sumac and the hummus is as smooth as cashmere. There's also baba ganoush, cinnamon-scented rice with shredded chicken, buttery couscous with squash, crispy falafel, and spanakopita made with a thick, almost bread-like dough. The most interesting dish may be the bright pinkish-purple puree of beets and walnuts, and it is totally addictive.

MARK: You know what— everyone in every city complains about traffic.

RECIPE

BEET
and walnut puree

Besides its amazing color, this dip is wonderful for its combination of earthy
ingredients. It's great with warm pita bread—or just with a spoon.

SERVES 4

1 cup walnuts

1 pound beets, trimmed, boiled
  or roasted, peeled, and cut
  into large chunks

½ cup olive oil

¼ cup water

2 tablespoons tahini

1 to 2 tablespoons lemon juice

Kosher salt

Pulse the walnuts in a food processor until coarsely chopped. Add the beets and pulse until a rough paste forms. Add the olive oil, water, and tahini and pulse a few times, just until combined. Add lemon juice and salt to taste.

ALBAICÍN: The Albaicín, a UNESCO World Heritage Site, is Granada's Old Town. The Alhambra is what draws tourists to Granada, but the Albaicín is part of what keeps them engaged. A neighborhood built on a hill, it offers great views of the Alhambra and is the perfect place to spend an afternoon wandering through old stone streets.

THE ALHAMBRA

For such a grand and important structure, the Alhambra has a way of blending in with its surroundings. In Arabic, Alhambra means "Red Palace," and it was named for the red clay that surrounds it. The trees growing on the grounds produce persimmons, pomegranates, and oranges—fruits native to this part of Andalucía. The arches throughout emphasize the natural light, and the intricate system of fountains and terraced waterways gives a constant feeling of being outside while inside. It's not all nature, though. The Alhambra rewards a close gaze: its intricate carvings and stonework are the stuff of art historical legend.

GWYNETH: The word *granada* translates as "pomegranate"—which explains the city's use of the fruit in its coat of arms and on lampposts, street signs, and the like. I ate the best pomegranate of my life from a tree at the Alhambra.

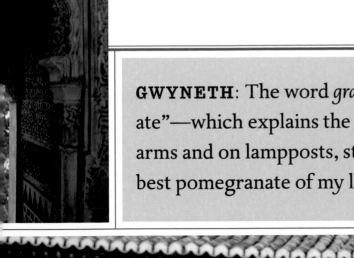

ALHAMBRA CHATTER

MARK: I didn't realize that the Alhambra was basically a water collection facility. So you would hang out here all summer, grow your *granadas* (pomegranates), eat your *granadas*, have some water fights . . .

GWYNETH: Sounds good to me.

MARK: There is everything here in this kitchen garden except potatoes and tomatoes, because those were New World. Oh, the life of a sultan [while eating a persimmon off a tree]. And what do you call a sultaness?

GWYNETH: Um, I think you just call it having multiple wives.

MARK: One of the things I love about you, Gwyneth, is that you eat first and you ask questions later.

GWYNETH: History be damned, I want to eat!

MARK: So the idea is that you would have four wives, one of whom would live in this tower.

GWYNETH: Does that idea appeal to you, Mark?

MARK: I wouldn't say it does or it doesn't.

GWYNETH: Imagine, you would have to go through menopause four times, Mark.

MARK: How is your cooking?

GWYNETH: My cooking gives me great joy. In the past few years, I've been home, I've been a mother, and I have been expressing myself creatively through food. I just sort of got in the habit of cooking all the time and reading a lot about it, and then I got really interested in how to make a really great meal, fresh, local, organic, in season, in a very short amount of time. So I would put the kids to bed and make a meal for the grown-ups. Which is an important part of life. I was thinking that would be an interesting book.

MARK: The "when the children are asleep" cookbook.

GWYNETH: Exactly, how to bathe them, put them to bed, lie with them until they fall asleep, and then make a great meal in forty minutes.

MARK: So whose cookbooks do you use, besides Mario's?

GWYNETH: I love Mario's books. I use the River Café cookbook a lot.

MARK: I always say there are four stages of learning how to cook. The first is you slavishly follow recipes; the second is you look through cookbooks, compare recipes, and pick one that makes sense to you; the third is you look at a bunch of recipes, then you walk away and cook something based on them but loosely; and the fourth is you don't think about recipes at all, you just take the ingredients and start cooking. The fourth is really liberating. You just look in the refrigerator or market and start cooking.

GWYNETH: I'd say I'm about halfway there.

MARK: Well, it's not that it's really a goal, it's an unconscious process. And you just get there at some point. What I find is that as I get older, I just keep cooking more simply; everything is getting simpler.

GWYNETH: Also, you feel good when you eat simply.

MARK: It's a lot easier to get really good ingredients.

GWYNETH: And not have to season and disguise them so heavily. Would you buy my cookbook?

MARK: Buy it? I'm going to write it for you.

FIDEOS
with seafood

At Restaurante Morayma, Esteban García Mingorance, a young chef, prepares traditional Andalucían food, like these fideos. Fideos are short pieces of thin pasta that are traditionally cooked like a rice pilaf—browned in oil, then cooked in only enough liquid to make them tender. You can use any type of seafood you like—whatever clams look best, whichever shrimp look freshest. The end result is a hearty, flavorful dish.

SERVES 6 TO 8

¼ cup extra-virgin olive oil

1 pound *fideos* (or substitute angel hair pasta broken into 1-inch pieces)

1 large onion, finely diced

2 garlic cloves, minced

1 teaspoon hot pimentón (Spanish smoked paprika)

One 28-ounce can whole peeled tomatoes

6 cups fish or seafood stock

1 cup dry white wine

1 bay leaf

A large pinch of saffron threads

1 pound mussels, scrubbed

1 pound medium shrimp in the shell

1 pound clams, scrubbed

Heat the oil in a large heavy pot over medium heat. Add the *fideos* and cook, stirring frequently, for about 10 minutes, or until well browned. Using a skimmer, transfer the *fideos* to a bowl. Add the onion, garlic, and pimentón to the pot and cook until the onion is beginning to soften, about 5 minutes. Add the tomatoes, breaking them up with your hands as you do so, and their juice, raise the heat to high, and cook, stirring frequently, until the tomatoes have broken down and the sauce has thickened, 15 to 20 minutes.

Meanwhile, combine the stock, wine, bay leaf, and saffron in another large heavy pot and bring to a boil. Add the seafood, cover, and cook for 4 to 6 minutes, or until all the clams and mussels have opened and the shrimp are opaque. Transfer the seafood to a large bowl and add the shellfish cooking liquid and *fideos* to the tomato sauce. Add the fideos and cook, stirring frequently, until the *fideos* have absorbed a lot of the liquid and are soft, 10 to 15 minutes. Add the shellfish, simmer gently just to heat through, and serve.

FAVORITE MOMENTS

GWYNETH: Looking back, what are some of your favorite moments from the trip?

MARK: Every time I try to think of a favorite moment, I am freezing to death in the back of a convertible.

CLAUDIA: I have too many. I loved the *mariscadoras* in Galicia. What about you?

GWYNETH: Gosh, there have been so many, but I really loved the Jewish Quarter of Girona.

MARK: We are going to have *La Gran Naranja* back in a few days. And I won't make any more pumpkin jokes.

GWYNETH: Did you liken him to a pumpkin?

MARK: A big orange thing? Yeah . . .

MARK: *Tengo un poquito de hambre* (I'm a little hungry).

CLAUDIA: You can have some of my fish, would you like some of my sole?

MARK: That's okay, I have some of your soul already.

TEJERINGOS: In addition to Spanish and English, I speak a few other languages, Swedish among them. There's a great Swedish word, *lagom*, which has no exact translation in English. Basically, though, it indicates sufficiency, the satisfaction of something being just right. Well, *tejeringos*, a sort of *churro*, are totally *lagom*. They are, in fact, the royalty of the *churro* world—not too salty or sweet or heavy. Just perfect. Just *lagom*. —**CLAUDIA**

TEJERINGOS

Tejeringos are a lot like churros—Spain's delightful addition to the doughnut world. They should be super-crispy, so be patient and let them really brown.

MAKES ABOUT 12 TEJERINGOS

8 tablespoons (1 stick) unsalted butter, cut into 8 pieces

1 tablespoon sugar, plus about 1 cup for dusting

Pinch of salt

1 cup all-purpose flour

3 large eggs

8 cups extra-virgin olive oil, for deep-frying

Combine 1 cup water, the butter, sugar, and salt in a small heavy saucepan and bring to a boil, stirring occasionally until the butter melts. Turn the heat to low, add the flour (in one shot), and stir vigorously until the mixture forms a ball. Remove from the heat and add the eggs one at a time, stirring constantly. Transfer to a bowl and allow the batter to rest for 10 minutes in the refrigerator.

Meanwhile, heat 3 inches of olive oil to 365°F in a large heavy pot. Transfer the dough to a pastry bag fitted with a large star tip. Pipe 4-inch-long strips of dough into the hot oil, without crowding, and cook for 4 to 5 minutes, or until golden brown. Drain on paper towels, and repeat with the remaining batter. Dust generously with sugar and serve.

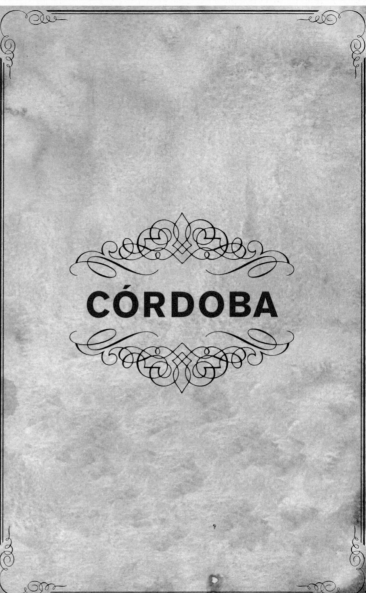

CÓRDOBA

Between the eighth and eleventh centuries, Córdoba was one of the world's most important centers of education, culture, and art. Its libraries held nearly half a million volumes, and Jews, Christians, and Moors lived together peacefully. In 1009, Omeyan and Prince Muhammad II triggered a rebellion that led to the spreading of Moorish power. Flash-forward about a thousand years, and find a city whose important past has been beautifully preserved. The Jewish Quarter's small streets make for reflective walking, the Mezquita's arches are still sturdy, and the Medina Azahara ruins are in remarkable shape.

ALCAZAR DE LOS REYES

In the fifteenth century Catholic monarchs held court in this fortress, built in 1328 by Alfonso XI. But then came the dark period: the fortress served as headquarters for the Spanish Inquisition for almost three hundred years. Boabdil was encarcerated here in 1483.

¿QUÉ es? **BOABDIL**: Boabdil, sometimes called "The Boy King," was Granada's last Moorish ruler. He's perhaps most famous, or infamous, for the story surrounding his exile. Apparently his mother told him that he should "weep like a woman for what [he] couldn't defend like a man." In fact, the place where Boabdil looked at Granada for the final time is called *"el último suspiro del Moro"* (the last sigh of the Moor).

¿QUÉ es? **CHERIMOYA**: A cherimoya, sometimes called a custard apple, is an oval fruit with soft, fragrant flesh. Mark Twain called it "deliciousness itself," and Claudia proclaimed it gorgeous. Its flavor is sort of like a mixture of mild pineapple, kiwi, and strawberry. Don't eat the seeds.

· RESTAURANT ·
SOCIEDAD DE PLATEROS
· CÓRDOBA ·

Sociedad de Plateros is from a bygone time. Located in a closed-in courtyard where servicemen used to come to eat and talk, this pseudo-canteen fed many, and it fed them cheaply and, more important, well. Now it's open to the public.

For lunch, *salmorejo*—a puree of tomatoes, bread, garlic, and olive oil garnished with chopped hard-boiled eggs and diced *jamón*. It's sort of like thick gazpacho and it's especially delicious alongside crispy fried *berenjena* (eggplant). Next comes pork *flamenquines*—pork wrapped around *jamón*, breaded, and deep-fried and served with mayonnaise and French fries. To end with a bang, *rabo de toro*, or stewed bull's tail. All very traditional.

RECIPE

FRIED EGGPLANT

When you fry it—fry it properly, that is—eggplant becomes really crispy on the outside and very creamy on the inside. It's an addictive snack—almost a variation of French fries—and goes really well with salmorejo. Like other Spanish fried foods, this is especially good because it uses great Spanish olive oil.

SERVES 4

6 to 8 cups extra-virgin olive oil, for deep-frying

2 large eggs

1 cup dried bread crumbs

1 large eggplant, cut into 3-inch-long, ½-inch-thick sticks (with the skin)

Coarse sea salt

Heat the olive oil to 365°F in a large deep skillet. Beat the eggs in a wide shallow bowl. Put the bread crumbs in another shallow bowl. Working in batches, dip the eggplant in the eggs and then in the bread crumbs, turning to coat, and add to the hot oil, without crowding. Fry until golden brown, about 5 minutes. Drain on paper towels, sprinkle with salt, and serve.

RECIPE

SALMOREJO

Salmorejo is somewhere between a soup and a sauce, sort of a dip. Like a very thick tomato gazpacho, it is served throughout Andalucía. It's great with fried eggplant, but it's equally good ladled over sliced of bread or, of course, eaten with a spoon. Traditionally it's topped with diced hard-boiled eggs and serrano ham.

SERVES 4

1 pound ripe tomatoes, cored
    and coarsely chopped

2 garlic cloves, minced

2 teaspoons sherry vinegar

¼ cup extra-virgin olive oil

2 cups ½-inch cubes stale bread
    (crusts removed)

Kosher salt

2 large hard-boiled eggs, peeled
    and finely chopped or pressed
    through a coarse sieve

¼ pound *jamón serrano* (you
    can substitute prosciutto),
    finely diced

Combine the tomatoes, garlic, vinegar, and olive oil in a blender or food processor and process to a puree. Add the bread in 2 batches and process until very smooth. Add salt to taste. Serve in shallow bowls, garnished with the eggs and ham.

CLAUDIA: I don't need Prozac. All I need is olive oil.

RECIPE

RABO DE TORO

I substituted oxtails for the traditional bull's tail, since they are more available.
If you have bull's tail, though, by all means use it!

SERVES 6

¼ pound slab bacon,
    cut into ½-inch cubes
3 ½ pounds oxtails,
    cut into 2-inch pieces
1 large Spanish onion,
    cut into ½-inch dice
3 carrots, cut into ¼-inch dice
3 stalks celery, thinly sliced
5 sprigs thyme
5 garlic cloves, crushed
    and peeled
Kosher salt and freshly ground
    black pepper
1 cup dry white wine
One 14-ounce can whole
    peeled tomatoes
1 bay leaf

Cook the bacon in a pot large enough to hold the oxtails in one layer over medium heat until the fat is rendered and the bacon is crisp. Using a slotted spoon, transfer the bacon to a plate. Add the oxtails to the fat remaining in the pot and cook, stirring occasionally, for about 30 minutes, until well browned all over. Transfer the oxtails to a tray and add the onion, carrots, celery, thyme, and garlic to the pot. Season with salt and pepper and cook for about 5 minutes, or until the vegetables are beginning to soften. Add the wine and bring to a boil, then lower the heat to a simmer. Return the oxtails and bacon to the pot, then add the tomatoes, breaking them up with your hands as you do so, along with their juices, and the bay leaf.

Cover the pot, transfer to a 300°F oven, and cook for 1 hour. Add a bit of water to the pot if it seems dry, cover, and cook for another hour. Check again, and cook for another hour, or until the meat is falling-apart tender.

RECIPE

FLAMENQUINES

For a while, Mark kept calling this dish "pork flamingo," pretending it had something to do with lawn ornaments. Anyway, it's good—similar to chicken Cordon Bleu, but with a less pretentious name. It's always served with mayonnaise and French fries—a platter of health if ever there was one.

SERVES 6

Six 3-ounce boneless pork loin chops

6 thin slices *jamón serrano* (you can substitute prosciutto)

2 large eggs

1 tablespoon water or milk

1 cup dried bread crumbs

Olive oil for shallow-frying

Mayonnaise and lemon wedges for serving

Place each piece of pork between 2 sheets of plastic wrap and, using a meat mallet, pound to ¼ inch thick. Lay a slice of ham on each piece of pork, roll up into a tight cylinder, and secure with a couple of toothpicks. Beat the eggs with the water in a shallow bowl. Put the bread crumbs in another shallow bowl. Dip each pork roll into the eggs and then into the bread crumbs, turning to coat; set aside on a plate.

Heat ½ inch of oil in a large skillet to 375°F over medium-high heat. Add the pork rolls and cook, turning occasionally, until golden and crisp on all sides, about 10 minutes total. Drain on paper towels, then cut into 1-inch slices and serve.

MEDINA AZAHARA

A bout five miles west of Córdoba, the ruins at Medina Azahara are a mind-boggling trip to a Muslim palace built over a period of twenty-five years, starting in 936 (it was destroyed by Berber mercenaries in 1013). The palace was commissioned by Abd ar-Rahman III and is said to have taken the labor of 10,000 men, 400 camels, and 2,600 mules. A bit of a fantasy land, it supposedly had almost 4,500 columns in green, white, and pink marble and quartz.

FAVORITE FRIED FOOD

GWYNETH:

ANYTHING AND EVERYTHING.

MARIO:

ARTICHOKES.

CLAUDIA:

ARTICHOKES.

MARK:

I'll go with the perfect **FRENCH FRY.**

WHAT WE'RE LOOKING FORWARD TO

There's a restaurant in Valladolid where I had an incredible meal—I told Claudia and Mark that they have to go on their travels into Castilla y León. They promise they will, and they'll also report back from Salamanca and Segovia.

8

From SALAMANCA to SEGOVIA

WHERE WE'RE GOING

This region is known for simple, modest cooking based on great ingredients. This is often the best kind of food, as the ingredients get to just sing—La Criolla's *lechazo* and Mesón de Cándido's *cochinillo* are great examples. Claudia and Mark fared well even without Gwyneth and me. When I return to Spain, they tell me all about incredible architecture, roasted pig, and not a small amount of great red wine.

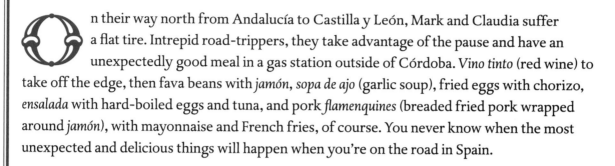

On their way north from Andalucía to Castilla y León, Mark and Claudia suffer a flat tire. Intrepid road-trippers, they take advantage of the pause and have an unexpectedly good meal in a gas station outside of Córdoba. *Vino tinto* (red wine) to take off the edge, then fava beans with *jamón*, *sopa de ajo* (garlic soup), fried eggs with chorizo, *ensalada* with hard-boiled eggs and tuna, and pork *flamenquines* (breaded fried pork wrapped around *jamón*), with mayonnaise and French fries, of course. You never know when the most unexpected and delicious things will happen when you're on the road in Spain.

RECIPE

FAVA BEANS
with ham

You can also make this dish with fresh fava beans—shell them, boil them, slip off their skins, and just add them at the end of the recipe. Labor-intensive, tedious work, to be sure—but fresh favas are worth it. Get someone to help you, and it'll go that much quicker.

SERVES 8 TO 10 AS A TAPA

1 pound dried peeled fava beans, soaked overnight in water to cover

3 tablespoons extra-virgin olive oil

1 small yellow onion, finely diced

1 garlic clove, minced

3 ounces *jamón serrano*, finely diced (you can substitute prosciutto)

Drain the beans, put them in a large pot, and add water to cover by 2 inches. Bring to a boil, then lower the heat and simmer gently for 1½ hours, or until tender. Drain, reserving 1 cup of the cooking liquid, and set aside.

Heat the oil in a large sauté pan over medium heat. Add the onion and garlic and cook, stirring frequently, for 7 to 10 minutes, or until softened. Add the ham and cook for 2 minutes, or until it begins to brown. Add the beans and the reserved cooking liquid and cook for 10 minutes, or until the beans have absorbed most of the liquid. Serve hot.

SOPA DE AJO
(garlic soup)

Really simple, really satisfying, really good. This may seem like a throwaway recipe, but follow the ingredients list and steps exactly, and you will wonder why you have all of those celebrity chef cookbooks in your kitchen.

SERVES 6

¼ cup olive oil

½ pound stale bread,
   crusts removed and cut into
   ½-inch cubes (about 3 cups)

8 garlic cloves, finely minced

1 teaspoon hot pimentón
   (Spanish smoked paprika)

Kosher salt

8 cups chicken stock,
   vegetable stock, or water

6 poached eggs

Heat the olive oil in a large saucepan over medium-high heat. Add the bread and cook, stirring, until golden brown, about 5 minutes. Add the garlic, pimentón, and a good pinch of salt. Cook for about 3 minutes, or until very fragrant. Add the stock and bring to a boil, then lower the heat and simmer for about 15 minutes, or until the bread is very soft. Taste and add salt if necessary. Ladle the soup into six bowls, put a poached egg into each, and serve.

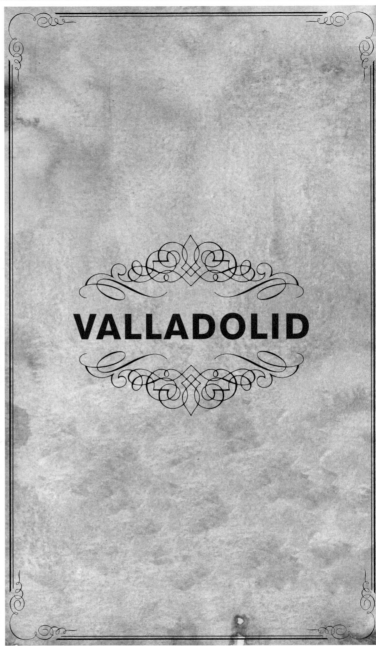

VALLADOLID

Valladolid is an industrial city in Ribera del Duero. Its name comes from the word "valley"—logical enough, seeing that it's in the valley of the Duero River. Valladolid was the birthplace of Philip II, who lived here until he left for Madrid in 1561. Other notable Valladolidians include Christopher Columbus, who died here in 1506, and Cervantes, who lived here for three years starting in 1603. Mark and Claudia dine at La Criolla, one of my favorite Castilla y León restaurants.

· RESTAURANT ·
LA CRIOLLA
· VALLADOLID ·

Paco Martínez is an Olympic chef: literally. He is the Spanish team's chef, and he wears his purple neckerchief like a flag. When pouring wine, he spins the glass in the air so quickly and with such control that it appears to be floating.

Paco serves Mark and Claudia a gratin of *bacalao* (salt cod) and vegetables, followed by *morcilla* (blood sausage) with wine-poached pears. Next are mushrooms with garlic, sherry, and nuggets of lamb sweetbreads, and then lamb kidneys with zucchini. Once the innards have been happily consumed, Paco returns to the kitchen to finish the *lechazo* (roasted baby lamb), but he leaves Mark and Claudia with a bowl of large white beans cooked simply with garlic, tomato, and olive oil. The dish exemplifies Paco's confidence. He is not afraid to present the simple, to celebrate the beauty of minimalism. To complement the humble beans, he brings out a bottle of Vega Sicilia 1972 wine. The *lechazo* makes its appearance with a lettuce, tomato, and onion salad. The lamb is succulent and even a bit sweet. You don't really need a knife eat it—the meat falls from the bones and from the crispy caramelized skin.

MARK: You did well when you ate the sweetbreads in Valladolid.

CLAUDIA: When I ate the what?!

VEGA SICILIA: Vega Sicilia is a vineyard in Ribera del Duero. When the chef presented Mark and Claudia with a bottle from 1972, they knew they were in for something sensational. Paco offered an old saying about the wine, which roughly translates as "whoever drinks a lot of this wine is allowed to screw even God."

STEWED BEANS

A chef who will serve stewed beans with a glass of 1972 Vega Sicilia knows that simple is best, that less is more, that understated is sophisticated.

SERVES 6

1 pound dried Corona beans (or other large white beans), soaked overnight in water to cover

2 garlic cloves, crushed and peeled

2 or 3 large ripe tomatoes, diced (or one 14-ounce can peeled whole tomatoes)

Kosher salt and freshly ground black pepper

Extra-virgin olive oil

Drain the beans, put in a large pot, and add the garlic and water to cover by 1 inch. Bring to a boil, then lower the heat to a simmer and cook, stirring occasionally, until the beans are soft, about 1½ hours; add more water if necessary to keep the beans covered.

Add the tomatoes (if using canned tomatoes, break them up with your hands as you add them) and a large pinch, or two or three, of salt and pepper. Cook for another 10 or 15 minutes, until the tomatoes have completely broken down. Serve drizzled with olive oil.

SALAMANCA

Salamanca was founded as a fort to defend the Roman territories. In 1218, Alfonso IX established the university, and the city quickly came to be one of the most significant academic centers in all of Europe. Students still make up a large percentage of the city's population, but it's not your average college town. The architecture is incredible—the buildings actually glow—and the narrow streets are perfect for wandering. Best is finding a seat in the main plaza and people watching while snacking on a plate of *churros*.

The plaza is classically Spanish. People sit and drink coffees, many of the men wear corduroy pants and hunting jackets, old women gossip—probably about the men—and students run back and forth to class. The architecture—with its archways and intricate stonework—is stunning and the sun is just right.

CHURROS and JAMÓN: *a winning combination*

Mark wanted *churros* and Claudia wanted *jamón*, so they had both. Little did they know that the combination would draw dubious looks and critical mumbles from their neighboring loungers in the Plaza Mayor. Apparently it's not appropriate to combine the two, but why settle for one when you can have both?

 VILLAMAYOR STONE: Salamanca is sometimes referred to as La Ciudad Dorada, or The Golden City, because of the special Villamayor stone. It's sandstone from a quarry in Villamayor, a nearby town. The golden color of the stone is sensational, and age has only improved it. Buildings blush in Salamanca, and one can't help but feel a bit luminous walking through the city.

 FIND THE FROG: In the classrooms of Salamanca's famous university, Columbus gave lectures about his explorations, Cortés studied geography, and Cervantes took courses in the humanities. We just came to look at the frog. The outside of one of the school's main buildings is ornately decorated in bas relief sculpture, and legend has it that the student who was able to spot the image of a frog without assistance did not have to take final examinations. Needless to say, it's now become a game among tourists. You'll find the frog . . . not!—as if I'd give that kind of information away. —**CLAUDIA**

Visiting Finca el Gejo let Claudia in on the secrets behind her favorite food of all time, *jamón*. The farm seems almost surreal, the famous black-footed pigs roaming through an endless landscape. The pigs eat only acorns, which explains the amazing flavor of the *jamón*, and they're each allotted a pretty decent piece of real estate to ensure that they have plenty of acorns. The branches of the trees create beautiful, almost spooky shadows and when Mark and Claudia arrive just before dusk, the light is perfect.

SEGOVIA

The name Segovia is said to come from the Celtic word for "fortress," and between the Roman aqueduct and the city walls, you can't help but feel the strength and brawn of the place. The incredible preservation of these ruins enabled the entire city to be protected and recognized as a UNESCO World Heritage Site. It's an extraordinarily beautiful city and makes for a perfect day trip from Valladolid.

¿QUÉ es?

AQUEDUCT: Segovia's aqueduct stands in the center of the city, and it is one of the most important and well preserved Roman monuments in Spain. It's constructed of more than 20,000 granite blocks that were fitted together without any mortar or even clamps. Mark summed up the experience of seeing it when he said simply, "I can't believe this is still standing."

MESÓN DE CÁNDIDO

Pretty much everyone in Segovia—residents and visitors alike—eats here. And they all eat the *cochinillo*, suckling pig. The owner, son of Cándido, the original owner, is known as the *mesonero mayor de Castilla* (major innkeeper of Castilla), and he can always be seen wearing his impressive medal. The restaurant is an old-fashioned place with distinctive customs—just the place to visit when you're on a food-obsessed, culture-curious road trip.

COCHINILLO ASADO

This is what you eat at Mesón de Cándido. Maybe a little green salad with raw onion, but otherwise don't even consult the menu. The skin of the suckling pig is so crisp that it can be famously shattered with a dinner plate.

SERVES 6, WITH LEFTOVERS

A handful of fresh bay leaves

1 suckling pig (about 12 pounds), cleaned

¼ pound high-quality lard, melted

4 garlic cloves, minced

Put the bay leaves in a large roasting pan and lay the pig on top, belly up. Add about a cup of water to the pan. Cook in a 350ºF oven for 30 minutes. Turn the pig over. Prick the skin all over with a sharp paring knife, then brush with the lard and rub with the garlic. Cook for another 30 minutes to 1 hour depending on the size of the pig, until the skin is very crispy and the meat is tender and succulent; a thermometer inserted in the shoulder should register 145°F. Let rest for 15 to 20 minutes.

Carve and serve, making sure each diner gets some of the cripy skin.

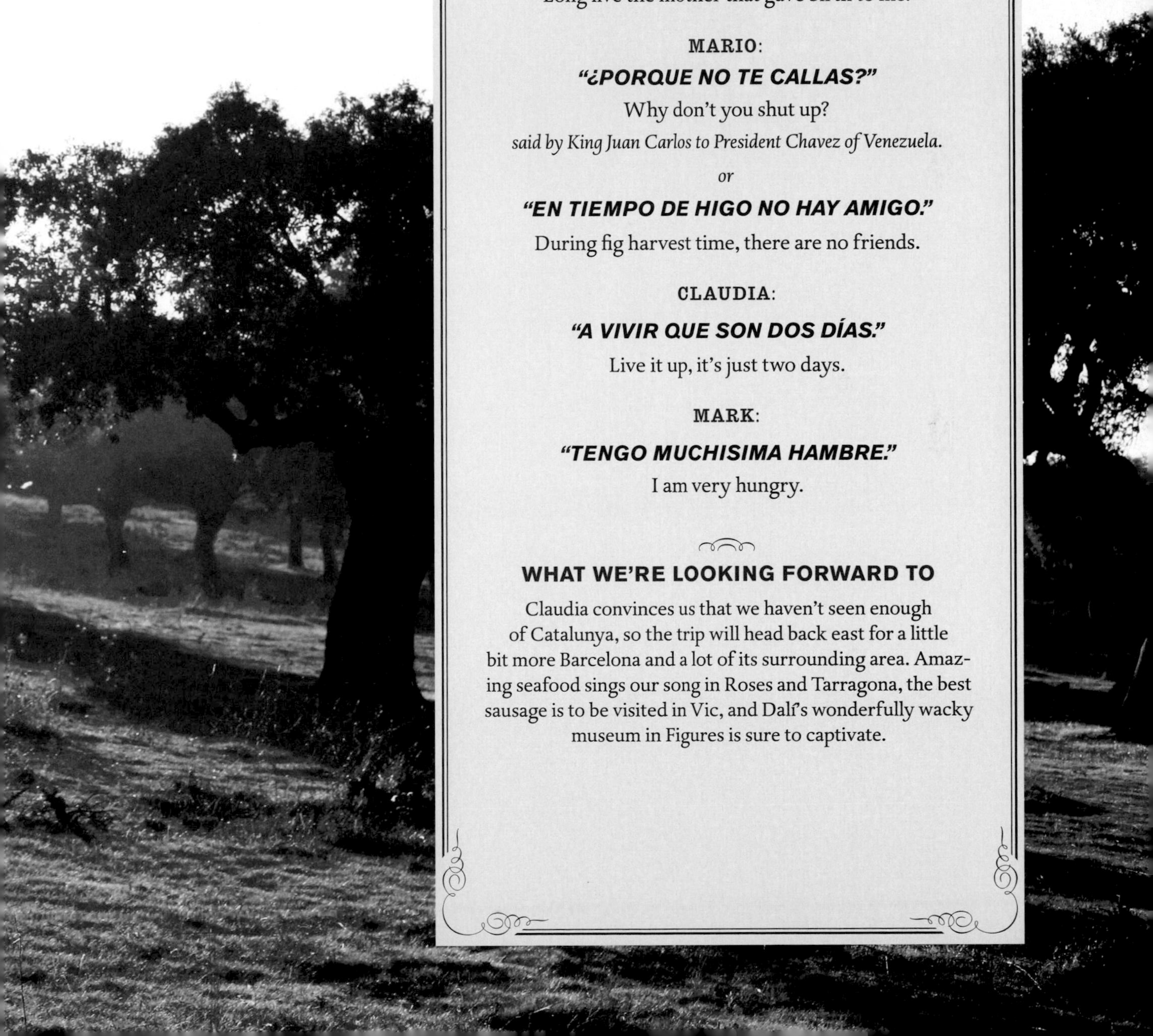

FAVORITE
SPANISH PHRASE

GWYNETH:

"¡VIVA LA MADRE QUE ME PARIO!"

Long live the mother that gave birth to me.

MARIO:

"¿PORQUE NO TE CALLAS?"

Why don't you shut up?

said by King Juan Carlos to President Chavez of Venezuela.

or

"EN TIEMPO DE HIGO NO HAY AMIGO."

During fig harvest time, there are no friends.

CLAUDIA:

"A VIVIR QUE SON DOS DÍAS."

Live it up, it's just two days.

MARK:

"TENGO MUCHISIMA HAMBRE."

I am very hungry.

WHAT WE'RE LOOKING FORWARD TO

Claudia convinces us that we haven't seen enough of Catalunya, so the trip will head back east for a little bit more Barcelona and a lot of its surrounding area. Amazing seafood sings our song in Roses and Tarragona, the best sausage is to be visited in Vic, and Dalí's wonderfully wacky museum in Figures is sure to captivate.

9

From SANT CARLES DE LA RÁPITA to ROSES

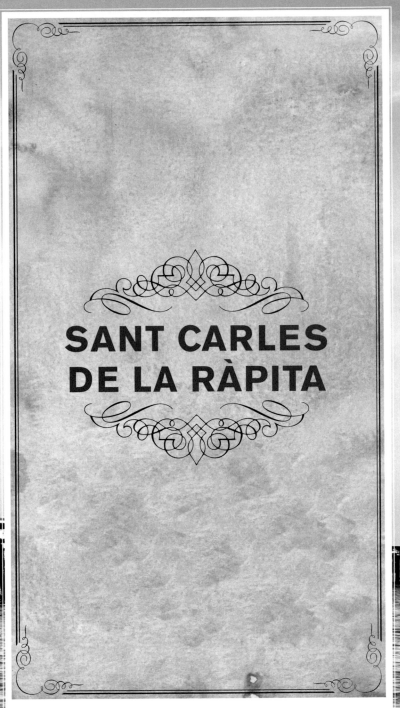

SANT CARLES DE LA RÀPITA

arragona, a port city in southern Catalunya, is about an hour from Barcelona. The mild Mediterranean climate helps make it a popular tourist destination, and the Disney-like theme park, Port Aventura, is also a draw. Instead of going for the roller coasters, though, Mark and Claudia head out for some fishing in Sant Carles de la Ràpita, south of Tarragona.

· THE SEA ·

ON THE WATER

· SANT CARLES DE LA RÀPITA ·

Mark and Claudia go out on a boat with Captain Ramón to gather oysters and mussels, and then they get to eat at a traditional *chiringuito*, basically a kiosk, but this one is on stilts. It is a wonderful morning on the water, and after lunch, they go to a fish auction. It smells like the sea. Plastic bins of fish come down a belt, and buyers press their hand buzzers to purchase a bin. One woman is working five buzzers—one for each restaurant she buys for.

CHIRINGUITO: A *chiringuito* is essentially a kiosk, or a snack bar, if you will. On the coast, though, *chiringuitos* are often built on stilts to protect them from the water, and they always serve the freshest seafood around— perfect beach food.

FIGUERES

Figueres is a bit north of Barcelona, near Girona. It's most famous as the birthplace of the renowned surrealist artist Salvador Dalí. Today it is also the site of the Teatre-Museu Dalí. The whole building—originally a theater—is a Dalí work of art, and it has been called "The World's Largest Surrealist Object." Dalí designed not just the pieces on the walls, but also the walls themselves—not to mention the fountains, statues, and ceilings. Something of a curiosity cabinet on steroids, the museum embodies Dalí's creative musings. Everything's kind of *loco*.

CADILLAC IN THE COURTYARD: One of the most well known works in the Dalí Museum is *The Rainy Cadillac*. General Motors only made a small number of these Cadillacs, and they gave them to Al Capone, Clark Gable, President Roosevelt, and Salvador Dalí, among others. The story goes that one day Dalí was standing in the rain waiting for a cab and decided that it should be the other way around. So he took his special Cadillac, installed three mannequins (to represent himself, his wife, and the driver), and rigged it so that when you insert a coin in the meter outside, it rains inside the car. Incredible.

ROSES

Roses is one of the largest towns on Catalunya's Costa Brava. It's quiet and relaxed and doesn't draw too much attention to itself—that is, of course, except for the hordes of people knocking on the door of El Bulli, Spain's most famous restaurant. El Bulli is closed for half the year, so when Mark and Claudia arrive in Roses in the fall, they head, on Ferran Adrià's own recommendation, to nearby Rafa's. Claudia says that if she lived in Roses, she'd go to Rafa's every day. Later during the trip when we all return to Madrid and meet up with Ferran, Mark and Claudia tell him all about their meal.

Ferran Adrià says that Rafa's, which, like his own El Bulli, in Roses, is the best place in the world to eat fish. He might be right. It's small—the restaurant has only five tables—and it's pretty perfect. Rafa runs the place with Rosa, a woman who came to Roses years ago to scuba dive and never left. When a gypsy read Rafa's palm, he was told he would live to be 169. He attributes it to good fish.

Speaking of good fish, Rafa doesn't open if he doesn't have it. His simple preparations are so good because his ingredients are so good. He works neatly and precisely, but is not at all "textbook." He is wonderfully intuitive—he knows the *gambas* (shrimp) are cooked when he smells the steam just barely beginning to turn to smoke. His sixth sense about food is something he can't explain.

First Rafa prepares two varieties of *chipirones* (baby squid), and presents them side by side to show their subtle differences. Then the *gambas*, cooked on a bed of salt. Next come whelks served with a laurel citronette. Finally *rubio*, white fish, cooked *a la plancha* and served with a garlic vinaigrette.

GRILLED FISH
with Garlic Vinaigrette

*This fish was perfectly cooked and the garlic in the dressing was crispy and delicious.
Claudia proclaimed it gorgeous.*

SERVES 2 GENEROUSLY

One 1-pound cod or other firm
    white fish fillet
1 tablespoon extra-virgin olive
    oil plus ½ cup
Coarse sea salt
8 garlic cloves, thinly sliced
¼ cup apple cider vinegar

Heat a *plancha* or a cast-iron skillet over a hot grill fire or
high heat until hot. Rub the fish with 1 tablespoon of the
oil and sprinkle with salt. Cook until golden brown on both
sides and opaque throughout, about 6 minutes per side.

Meanwhile, heat the remaining ½ cup olive oil in a
small skillet over medium-low heat. Add the garlic and
cook slowly until the garlic is golden brown and crisp,
being careful not to burn it. Add the vinegar (be careful,
as the oil may spit and pop) and stir to combine.

Transfer the fish to a platter, pour the vinaigrette,
with the garlic chips, over it, and serve.

RECIPE

GAMBAS
a la plancha

Rafa explains that he cooks the gambas (shrimp) on a bed of salt because it preserves their moisture and keeps them juicy. Whatever the reason, his were some of the best. Claudia eats only the shrimp bodies, and Mark loves the heads—like Jack Sprat and his wife, they make a good team.

SERVES 2 TO 3

Coarse sea or kosher salt

1 pound large head-on shrimp
  in the shell

Heat a *plancha* or large cast-iron skillet over a hot grill fire or medium-high heat until hot. Spread a ¼-inch-thick layer of salt on the *plancha* (or in the skillet). Lay the shrimp on the salt and cook until opaque throughout, 2 to 3 minutes per side. Serve with plenty of napkins.

WHELKS
with Citronette

Simple and delicious, my kind of cooking. Whelks, also known as sea snails and called scungilli in Italian, are a delicious, funky mollusk. They look like small conch and taste a bit like snails. Try them if you see them.

To get the whelks out of their shells can be a bit tricky. Use a little lobster fork, or even a metal skewer.

SERVES 2 TO 3

1 pound whelks, scrubbed

6 fresh bay leaves

3 tablespoons extra-virgin olive oil

Juice of 1 lemon

Bring a large pot of generously salted water to a boil. Add the whelks and 3 of the bay leaves, reduce the heat slightly, and boil gently for 30 minutes. Drain and run the whelks under cold water to cool them.

Warm the olive oil in a small saucepan over medium heat. Add the remaining 3 bay leaves and cook for a minute or two, until fragrant. Pour the olive oil into a small bowl, leaving the bay leaves behind. Add the lemon juice and mix together with a fork. Serve the whelks with the citronette.

VIC

Vic, a bit north of Barcelona, is on the Méder River. It's a small city with a beautiful historic quarter that's dominated by the cathedral, which is known for its murals. All you need is a quick walk around the city to feel comfortable. Claudia and I came especially for the *salchichón* and *fuet*—two dried sausages Vic is known for. Claudia is a *fuet* addict and has been for her entire life. She says her father used to buy one, peel off its casing, and cut it into thin slices, and they would proceed to eat the entire thing, just the two of them (not a small feat).

CASA RIERA ORDEIX

We're here in Vic to visit Casa Riera Ordeix, where they've been making *salchichón* since 1852. Located in the Plaza Martires, the place looks like an apartment building from the outside, but inside there's a full-on USDA cleaning and chopping place with a 200-pound mixer, stirrer, and stuffer. Above this floor is a five-story curing room with vertiginous slatted floors and a consistent 40°F temperature.

The owners are nice guys, seventh generation in the business. The whole process begins on the first floor, where, on huge stainless steel tables, workers cut beautiful sides of pork into pieces the size of a deck of cards. They carefully remove the gristle, silverskin, nerves, and bones without sacrificing any meat. All the workers wear white coats and aprons, thick-soled shoes, and little train conductor hats. The production seems very handmade—the factory is quiet, just the noise of precise cutting. I ask everyone if they all still have ten fingers, and they laugh.

We move to the next part of production, the grinding and stuffing. The meat goes through a large metal grinder and then is mixed with salt, pepper, and bacon. After it rests for forty-eight hours, it is stuffed into casings, poked with a pin to drain out water or release air pockets, and then taken upstairs to one of the curing rooms to age for four or five months. The workers can tell when it's ready just by touching it. Claudia says that the curing room is her paradise and that she just wants to dive in. As for me, I'm happy just to snack.

¿QUÉ es?

CASINGS: What holds that meat in? Well, to be blunt, intestines. Sausage casings are made from something called the submucosa, a specific layer of the intestine. It works because it's made up of collagen—a firm, flexible protein (which is also why it's used for certain plastic surgeries).

We find an amazing restaurant in Vic, Can Jubany. It's run by Nando Jubany and is in a beautifully renovated fifteenth-century farmhouse. Our meal there is stunning.

I love the place immediately because Nando brings out a salami "in case we get hungry while we wait for the next plate." It's a bit like when chef Paco Martínez served his plain but beautiful beans with a Vega Sicilia wine at La Criolla in Valladolid, and we noted the confidence it takes for a chef to drop a great salami on the table and just leave it there, not trying to compete with it—especially a chef whose food is so spectacular and layered. Our first dish is a shrimp tartare with potatoes, sweet tomatoes, sturgeon caviar, and a tiny quail egg on top. It's barely acidic, a little sweet, and very sophisticated. Next is Catalan puff pastry filled with foie gras, caramelized figs, and tomato confit, with a sweet wine reduction. Then we have slow-roasted bacon with morcilla (blood sausage) and mushrooms—it's a rich, meaty dish, and perfectly cooked. To balance it, our next course is a paella-style rice with *espardeñas* (sea cucumbers) and langostino broth; it's light and delicate. Our fifth course (we didn't realize what we had signed on for) is cod baked in a wood oven with potatoes, Catalan country sausage, and egg. It's honest, good food made quite elegant. Our sixth and final savory course is an amazing chicken that's been cooked for twelve hours at 190°F, served with sautéed cauliflower and a rich foie gras and chicken liver sauce. For dessert, we have a variety of chocolate sweets and then a sweet orange something or other. Throughout the entire meal, Claudia snacks on the salami and, as we finish, I tell her there's room for her in my family—anyone who eats salami with their chocolate is an honorary Batali.

MARIO: For me this meal is like my birthday—all things I like, made by someone else.

slow-roasted
CHICKEN

Nando cooks his chicken for twelve hours because his birds are strong, flavorful, free-range, and somewhat tough. I cut the time a bit since our chickens aren't as tough—but they also aren't as wonderfully chickeny.

SERVES 4

¼ pound pancetta, cut into
    ¼-inch dice
¼ pound *butifarra* or other pork
    sausage, casings removed and
    cut into ¼-inch dice
One 3 to 4 pound chicken
2 cups chicken stock

Mix the pancetta and *butifarra* together, and stuff the cavity of the chicken with the mixture. Put the chicken in a heavy pot that holds it snugly, pour over the chicken stock, and cover the pot. Put the pot into a 200°F oven and cook for 6 hours. The chicken will be unbelievably tender.

BARCELONA

Since our first visit to Catalunya was really only to Barcelona, we came back to see Tarragona, Roses, Figueres, and Vic. But, because we were so close to Barcelona, Claudia couldn't resist bringing Mark and me back to her hometown one more time.

CAN PINEDA

Can Pineda is a perfect old-school restaurant. It's small and warm, and when you walk in, you know you're entering a place with years of experience under its belt. The guys who run the place are easygoing, fun, and full of personality. When the waiter realizes he forgot to bring us our wine, he rushes to fill our glasses and tells us a story about how someone in his hometown started eating without wine and then drowned. He's superstitious, for sure, but lively and quirky too. For a cook, it is particularly enjoyable to eat in a place with character, with soul, and most significant, where someone knows how to cook their balls off, and they do here.

TRIPE
with chile and bacon

A lot of people are freaked out by tripe, but it's really one of the best vehicles for an assertively flavored sauce. This recipe is a good example of tripe's ability to stand up to bold flavors.

SERVES 4

1 pound honeycomb tripe

¼ cup white vinegar

½ pound bacon, cut into
¼-inch dice

1 medium red onion, cut into
¼-inch dice

1 teaspoon chile flakes

One 28-ounce can whole
peeled tomatoes

Put the tripe in a large pot, add the vinegar and enough water to cover, and bring to a boil. Reduce the heat to a simmer and cook until the tripe is tender, about 1 hour. Remove from the heat and let the tripe cool in the cooking liquid, then drain and cut into 1-inch pieces.

Cook the bacon in a large skillet until the fat is rendered and the bacon is crisp. Add the onion and chile flakes and cook, stirring, for about 6 minutes, until the onion is beginning to soften. Add the tomatoes, breaking them up with your hands as you do so, along with their juices, and bring to a boil. Lower the heat, cover, and simmer gently for 20 minutes.

Add the tripe and bring to a boil, then lower the heat and simmer for another 20 minutes. Serve with crusty bread.

RICE
with lobster stock and mushrooms

A really delicious arroz. The combination of lobster stock and mushrooms is an especially savory one. If you like, you can fold in some cooked lobster meat at the end for a more luxurious dish.

SERVES 4

4 cups lobster stock (see Note)

1 cup bomba rice (you can substitute Arborio)

3 tablespoons extra-virgin olive oil

½ pound mixed wild mushrooms, trimmed as necessary

kosher salt and freshly ground black pepper

Heat the lobster stock in a small saucepan; keep warm over low heat. Set a medium heavy pot over medium heat, add the rice and 1 cup of the warm stock, and bring to a boil, then reduce the heat to a gentle simmer and cook, stirring, until the rice has absorbed most of the stock. Add another cup of stock and cook, stirring, until most of the stock has been absorbed. Continue to cook, stirring and adding stock each time the previous addition has had been aborbed, until the rice is tender; this will take about 20 minutes.

Meanwhile, heat the olive oil in a large sauté pan over high heat. Add the mushrooms and sauté for 5 to 8 minutes, or until browned and softened. Stir the mushrooms into the rice, season with salt and pepper to taste, and serve.

NOTE: For a quick lobster stock, cover lobster shells with water in a stockpot, add a handful of diced onion, carrot, and celery, and simmer for 30 minutes; strain through a fine-mesh sieve.

FAVORITE
CANDY BAR

GWYNETH:
PAYDAY

MARIO:
NESTLE'S CRUNCH

CLAUDIA:
FRUIT ROLL-UP

MARK:
MOUNDS

WHAT WE'RE LOOKING FORWARD TO

The trip becomes a boys-only event, as Claudia has auditions to go to and Gwyneth has a movie to shoot. Mark and I will head back up north to spend some time in Asturias, specifically to make some authentic *fabada*.

IO

From OVIEDO to COVADONGA

OVIEDO

Some say Oviedo, the biggest city in Asturias, was founded in 761 by two monks, Máximo and Fromestanus, but archaeologists have found Roman ruins there. Regardless, it's a beautiful, historic place and is one of the most important cities on the route to Santiago de Compostela (see Chapter Two). The historical center has a definite medieval feel to it and is dominated by a huge cathedral. It's an easy, comfortable city to walk, and it doesn't get much better than a few glasses of cider and a bowl of *fabada* in one of the old *sidrerías* (cider bars).

¿QUÉ es? **THE WOODY ALLEN THING**: You'll notice a certain fondness for Woody Allen in Oviedo—there's even a life-sized statue of him in the center of the city. We couldn't really figure it out at first, but we learned that he was the recipient of the Prince of Asturias Award in 2002. The awards, presided over by Felipe, Prince of Asturias, are an annual group of prizes given for achievement in science, humanities, and public affairs.

Camilo de Blas is a pastry shop and general store built in 1914. White shelves, glass-fronted cabinets, and deep drawers hold preserved whole peaches, cider, wine, chocolate, tinned fish, meringues, ice cream, nuts, meat pies, candies, *jamón*, anchovies, and *orujo* (the potent liquor), to name just a few things. When I say to the owner that there isn't a store like this in the United States, he replies, "There's not a store like this in Spain."

Among other items, they're very famous for pastries called *caballones*, named for the 600-year-old oak tree that used to stand in the middle of town but was cut down when they widened the streets in the 1940s—and has been mourned ever since. They consist of puff pastry in a tartlet shell with almond custard piped over the top, baked, cooled, and then dipped in a hot caramel bath. They remind me of the maple bars I used to love as a kid, and they are really good. But even more interesting are the savory empanadas—one with tuna, another chorizo, and a third with anchovies. We get a bunch of food for our car ride up to the mountains, with the result that by the time we arrive, to make hearty *fabada*, we're more ready for a siesta.

MAKING FABADA

¿QUIÉN es?

BEAN, the MULE WITHOUT A NAME: When we went up in the mountains to make *fabada* with Marco, Pedro, Nacho, and Estele (they're all related, but I still can't figure out how), there was a mule on the property. He was very cute and a bit skittish, and while the beans were cooking, we found out that he didn't have a name. And he's forty years old. We figured it was about time he got a name, so we called him Bean, in honor of the *fabada*.

You can't go to Asturias and not eat *fabada*. The region's most famous dish, *fabada* is a bean and pork stew, and Asturians are justly proud of it. In a way, the dish is emblematic of the area. Simple and a bit rugged, *fabada* lacks pretense but is full of assertive flavor. Asturias, in turn, is a coarse, rough, but totally unapologetic region. Its coast is lined with rocky cliffs, its mountains high and covered in lush greenery. It's often rainy and cold, foggy, and even a bit shadowy. Asturians are a hearty, healthy, robust people—no wonder, with all that mountain air and those steaming pots of *fabada*.

BOCADILLOS for a CAR RIDE

Here are some of our favorite *bocadillos*, sandwiches, to eat on a long car ride. Almost all sandwiches in Spain are served on soft rolls with a crunchy crust, unadorned by condiments or lettuce—it's just the bread and the main event. It would seem that they might be dry, but they never are.

OIL-PACKED TUNA *with thinly sliced raw onion and sliced hard-boiled egg*

SALCHICHON *from Vic*

TORTILLA ESPAÑOLA

GRILLED STEAK *with fried peppers*

MANCHEGO *with* membrillo *(quince paste)*

FRIED CALAMARI *with its own ink as a sauce (my personal fave)*

RECIPE

FABADA

Fabada is adored throughout Spain, and it should be adored throughout the world. It's an Asturian preparation of dried fabas (dried fava beans) of the granja (farm) variety and a whole slew of pork products. The similarity between fabada and cassoulet cannot be denied, especially when you consider Asturias's location on Spain's northern coast, so near to France. As with cassoulet, everyone's fabada is a bit different—a little more of this, a little more of that. This recipe is a good classic starting point.

SERVES 10 TO 12

2 pounds dried fava beans (from Asturias if possible), soaked overnight in water to cover

¼ cup extra-virgin olive oil

Pinch of saffron threads

1 tablespoon hot pimentón (Spanish smoked paprika)

1 head garlic, cut in half across the bulb

1 smoked ham hock

1 pound slab bacon

1 pound Spanish chorizo

1 pound *morcilla* (blood sausage)

1 onion, halved

Drain the beans. Put them in a large pot, add water to cover by 2 inches, and bring to a boil. Skim off any foam, lower the heat to a simmer, and add the olive oil, saffron, *pimentón*, garlic, ham hock, and bacon. Simmer for 1 hour, adding more water as necessary to keep the beans covered.

Add the chorizo, *morcilla*, and onion and simmer for another 2 hours, or until the beans are very soft; add water as necessary to keep the beans and meats covered. Remove from the heat, remove the meats, and let cool slightly.

Remove the meat from the ham hock and shred it into bite-sized pieces. Cut the bacon into 1-inch chunks and cut the sausages into thick slices. Discard the garlic and onion, ladle the beans into bowls, and nestle the various meats in the beans.

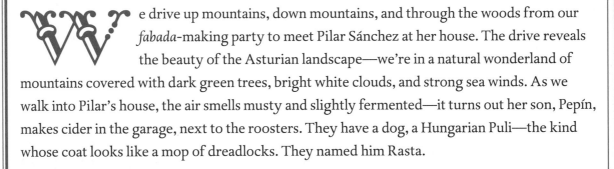

· GRANDMA'S HOUSE ·

CASA PEPÍN

· ASTURIAS ·

We drive up mountains, down mountains, and through the woods from our *fabada*-making party to meet Pilar Sánchez at her house. The drive reveals the beauty of the Asturian landscape—we're in a natural wonderland of mountains covered with dark green trees, bright white clouds, and strong sea winds. As we walk into Pilar's house, the air smells musty and slightly fermented—it turns out her son, Pepín, makes cider in the garage, next to the roosters. They have a dog, a Hungarian Puli—the kind whose coat looks like a mop of dreadlocks. They named him Rasta.

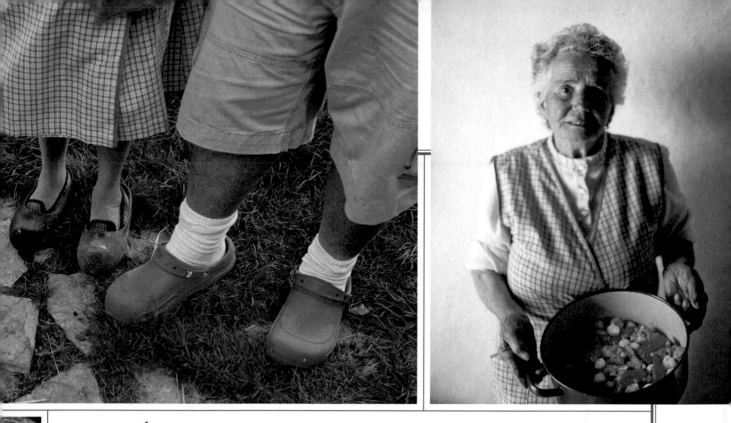

PILAR SÁNCHEZ

Pilar Sánchez is a short, sharp lady. Wearing her housedress, a sweater she knit herself, and plaid slippers, she welcomes us into her home and immediately offers us freshly roasted chestnuts. It seems that everything in the house is scaled to her size—the old wood-burning stove is low to the ground, the steps of the staircase are shallow, and Mark and I can barely stand up in the hallway. Pilar has lived in Asturias her entire life; the farthest away she's been is Madrid, which she's visited exactly four times. She loves coffee, especially in the morning after doing a "nice little sweep." She's in some ways the embodiment of the timeline of cooking in the twentieth century: she started out without running water and eating only what she had grown or raised; now she's comfortable shopping if necessary and even has a fryolator, and rather than canning things, as she used to, she now relies on her freezer. Still, though, as Mark put it, her main grocery store is the field she lives in. She cooks with the intuition and affection of a seasoned home cook and is, simply put, a perfect example of why I am here in Spain. The food we cook with Pilar sings of the region and the cook and has no tricks behind its magnificence.

PILAR'S CLOGS: When Pilar took us outside to show us her shepherd's hut, we couldn't help but notice that instead of putting on shoes, she just slipped on a pair of studded wooden clogs over her slippers. The "studs" on the bottoms, which make them sort of like miniature stilts, are purposeful—Asturias gets a lot of rain and the ground can be quite soggy, so Pilar's clogs are wonderfully functional. I showed her my clogs, and she seemed to like the orange color.

POLLO CASERO

Pollo casero *translates as "homemade chicken" and, in this instance, referred not only to the preparation of the dish, but also to the preparation of the chicken itself. When we asked Pilar where she got her chicken, she told us to go outside and listen—her chickens were the ones "singing" in the field below. She served this with little fried potato balls, but she wouldn't tell us how she made them; I'd suggest eating this with either small boiled potatoes or even French fries.*

SERVES 4

One 3½-pound chicken,
  cut into 8 pieces
2 garlic cloves, minced
1 tablespoon kosher salt
2 tablespoons olive oil
1 large onion, chopped
One 8-ounce jar pimento
  peppers
1 cup dry white wine

Rub the chicken all over with the garlic and salt. Cover and refrigerate for 1 hour.

Heat the oil over medium-high heat in a pot that will hold the chicken in a single snug layer. Working in 2 batches, add the chicken skin side down and brown very well on all sides, about 15 minutes per batch. Transfer the chicken to a platter.

Add the onion to the pot and cook for about 10 minutes, or until soft. Add the pimentos and wine, return the chicken to the pot, and bring to a simmer. Reduce the heat slightly, partially cover, and simmer for 1 hour, or until the chicken is very tender.

RECITE

BAKED APPLES

Pilar baked apples for dessert and they were soft and delicious. She gave us some to try in their raw state and they were incredibly crisp—almost too hard. They came, unsurprisingly, from her backyard. Use the crispest apples you can find; Macouns or Crispins would be good options. These are especially good with sour cream, ice cream, or even yogurt.

SERVES 6

6 crisp apples
2 tablespoons sugar
A small glass of cider
   (about ½ cup)

Core, but do not peel, the apples and put in a shallow baking dish. Sprinkle with the sugar and cider. Bake in a 375°F oven for about 1 hour, or until very soft. Serve hot, at room temperature, or cold.

¿QUÉ es? **GAMONEU:** Pilar took Mark and me into her shepherd's hut with her son, Pepín. It seemed as if she was going to tell us a secret and, as it turns out, she did. She told us about gamoneu, an Asturian cheese made with milk from sheep, goats, and cows. Thankfully, she also gave us a taste. Only seven shepherds in the world make it! It's famous in Asturias, but no one else seems to know about it—it seems Asturians eat it all. It's an extraordinary cheese, a full-flavored, white, and creamy cheese with a center that is blue-veined and wonderfully funky, definitely two cheeses in one. Two great cheeses in one.

RECIPE

ROASTED CHESTNUTS

Chestnuts, castañas in Spanish, grow all over Asturias in the fall. Pilar collects them around her house, roasts them, and keeps them warm wrapped in a tea towel for visitors. They're a good thing to peel and eat when you're sitting in the kitchen talking shop.

SERVES 4

1 pound chestnuts, preferably from your own trees

Spread the chestnuts on a baking sheet. (To make peeling them easier, you can cut an X in the flat side of each chestnut with a sharp paring knife.) Roast in a 450°F oven, turning every 5 minutes or so, for 15 minutes, or until the shells can be easily removed. Serve hot.

Covadonga is an Asturian village in the Picos de Europa, famous as the site of a legendary battle the Christians won over the Moors in 722. It was their first significant victory against the invaders and the beginning of the 700-or-so years of constant warring between the two sides. Standing near the statue of Pelayo, the ruler of the Asturian kingdom who initiated the battle and therefore the entire *reconquista*, Mark looked out at the landscape and remarked, "So the hill must've been their biggest ally." Could be.

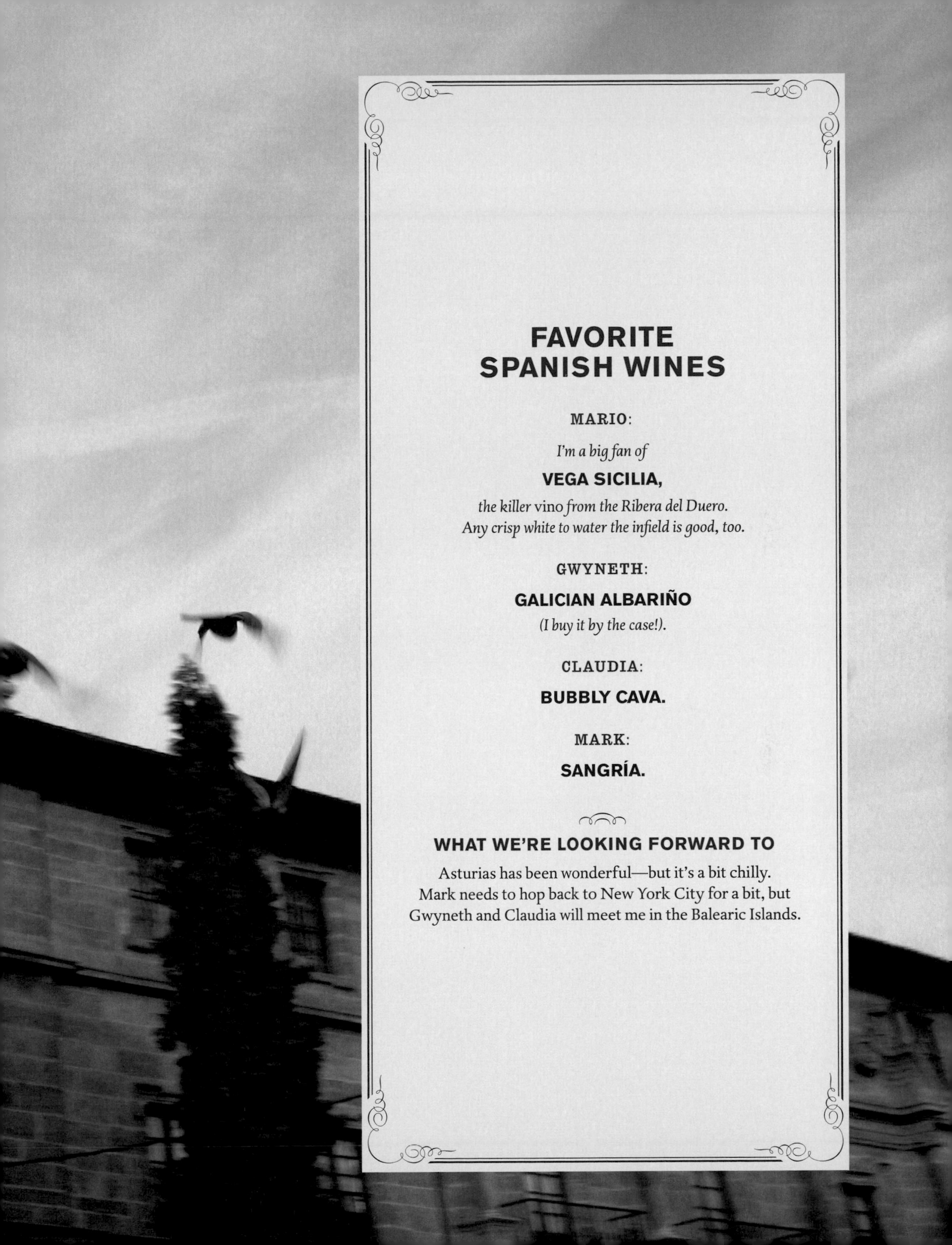

FAVORITE SPANISH WINES

MARIO:

I'm a big fan of
VEGA SICILIA,
*the killer vino from the Ribera del Duero.
Any crisp white to water the infield is good, too.*

GWYNETH:

GALICIAN ALBARIÑO
(I buy it by the case!).

CLAUDIA:

BUBBLY CAVA.

MARK:

SANGRÍA.

WHAT WE'RE LOOKING FORWARD TO

Asturias has been wonderful—but it's a bit chilly.
Mark needs to hop back to New York City for a bit, but
Gwyneth and Claudia will meet me in the Balearic Islands.

II

From MALLORCA to MENORCA

MALLORCA

The Balearic Islands, Mallorca (Majorca) and her neighbors Menorca, Ibiza, Formetera, and Cabrera, lie off the eastern coast of Spain and have been inhabited by human beings for six thousand years (that's Paleolithic times for you history buffs). In Roman times, Mallorca was famous for its grapevines and olives, but salt mining was the real cash cow. It has long been desirable both for its agricultural potential and, to pirates as well as commercial sailors, for its excellent position at the entrance of the Mediterranean. But I rush forward . . . Mallorca was seized by the Vandals and then by the Byzantines (as is almost traditional in coastal Iberia), then conquered in the early tenth century by the Moors and then reconquered by the Aragon crown under King James I in the mid-thirteenth century. When the Castile and Aragon crowns were united under the Catholic king and queen, Ferdinand and Isabella, Mallorca supported the new unity, but at the same time maintained a separate identity, and this "keep to itself" attitude still exists today. The capital is Palma de Mallorca, a beautiful town that hosts some of the Mediterranean's finest yachts, and has become a natural locale for assembling crew and supplies for sailing, always vibrant, and a little suspicious even now.

Felipe Jordi, the hippest businessman in Mallorca, lives in a modern apartment complete with Eames chairs and a floating staircase. Every Wednesday he hosts a private gourmet and wine club, the 12 Sybarites (kind of like the opposite of the twelve apostles), and each week the guest chef changes. We are lucky to be there when Benet Vicens is the chef for the evening. Benet is an extraordinarily happy man and takes wonderful joy in the preparation of food. As we cook together, I turn to him at one point and we acknowledge that we're not working, we're having dinner with our friends. This contentment prevails—everyone's happy to be here, happy to be together eating great but not-too-complicated food. It reminds me that the best food is often served at home, not in a restaurant.

We start with a refreshing carpaccio of incredibly sweet Mallorcan shrimp, garnished with a few greens and pine nuts and a scoop of basil sorbet. Benet offers me a few special salts made in Mallorca—one with hibiscus, another with black olive. It becomes clear that Mallorca, even in all of its simple pleasures, still pushes food to the Spanish edge. Next we prepare a crazy wonderful dish, a *frito* (fry) of lamb heart and liver with vegetables. Our final dish is a traditional pan of *fideos* with calamari, simple, but utterly sophisticated. Benet didn't necessarily plan to use the ink, but when his knife punctured the sac and the ink covered our hands, we figured, "Why not?"

Felipe, the consummate bachelor, gives a single rose to each woman, and another bottle of wine is opened. We end the night full and smiling, delighted to be hanging Mallorca-style.

CARPACCIO
de gambas

This dish really sang. The gambas (prawns) were fresh and sweet and the olive oil, local from Mallorca, was killer—all the taste and viscosity of a strong Tuscan. Benet conceptualized this dish twenty-three years ago after seeing a fisherman pop a raw shrimp into his mouth. Freshness is, indeed, vital—only make this dish when you can get very fresh, very sweet shrimp. Felipe chose a Moscatel to match the dish, because its acidity and sweetness mirrored that of the gambas. Claudia described each bite as a "festival for the mouth."

SERVES 4

1 pound fresh Santa Barbara spot prawns, the largest available (you can substitute Dublin Bay prawns or, if you are in Spain, Carabineros)

7 tablespoons extra-virgin olive oil

2 tablespoons toasted pine nuts

8 basil leaves, sliced into chiffonade (thin slivers)

Grated zest and juice of 1 lemon

1 cup arugula

Mallorcan (or Maldon) sea salt and freshly ground black pepper

Peel the shrimp, devein, and butterfly them down the back. Open out 2 shrimp, place between two sheets of plastic wrap, and gently pound with a meat mallet to flatten. Arrange the flattened shrimp on a serving plate and repeat with the remaining shrimp to make 4 servings. Drizzle 1½ tablespoons of the olive oil over each plate of shrimp. Scatter the pine nuts, basil, and lemon zest over them, and sprinkle with the lemon juice. Toss the arugula with the remaining 1 tablespoon oil and arrange on the shrimp. Sprinkle with salt and pepper and serve.

FRITO MALLORQUÍN

Claudia looked over our shoulders to see what we were making, then said, "I was going to ask what's in it, but I don't want to know." Clearly a sign that I would love this dish. Lamb heart and liver are combined with vegetables, garlic, bay leaves, and chile pepper. Felipe picked out a red wine heavy on tannins, structure, and body; it cut the fat of the dish and was another example of how a good wine and food pairing makes a sum greater than its parts.

SERVES 4

Heart from a young lamb
   (about 10 ounces),
   cut into ½-inch dice
Liver from a young lamb (about 1
   pound), cut into ½-inch dice
Mallorcan (or Maldon) sea salt
   and freshly ground
   black pepper
¼ cup extra-virgin olive oil
4 garlic cloves, thinly sliced
1 corno di bue chile or jalapeño,
   finely chopped
2 fresh bay leaves
2 large scallions, finely sliced
1 Yukon Gold potato, peeled
   and cut into 1-inch-long
   matchsticks
2 large artichoke hearts,
   cut into ¼-inch-wide slices
   and reserved in acidulated
   (lemon) water (see Note)
½ cup snow peas, cut in half
   on the diagonal
½ cup fennel fronds

Season the heart and liver aggressively with salt and pepper. Heat the oil in a large sauté pan over medium heat. Add the heart and liver and cook, stirring, until light golden brown, 7 to 8 minutes. Transfer to a bowl.

Add the garlic, chile, bay leaves, scallions, potatoes, and drained artichokes to the pan and cook until the artichokes and potatoes are softened, about 15 minutes.

Return the meats to the pan and stir for about 2 minutes, to warm through. Add the snow peas and cook for 3 minutes, until quite soft. Stir in the fennel fronds, and serve.

NOTE: To trim artichokes to hearts, cut off the stem from each one (as you work, rub the cut surfaces with a lemon half to prevent oxidation). Snap off the tough outer leaves until you reach the pale yellow cone of inner leaves. Cut off the cone of leaves and pull away the purple leaves surrounding the choke. Using a small sharp spoon, scoop out the fuzzy choke. Trim the dark green parts from the artichoke bottom.

FIDEOS
with calamari

The crucial thing about cooking a proper pan of fideos is texture—it's all based on liquidity. Benet added more fish stock than I had anticipated, but it worked because he had browned the noodles so thoroughly. The drier they are, the more they drink. For this, Felipe chose a light rosé whose freshness and acid absolutely complemented the dish.

SERVES 8

¼ cup plus 2 tablespoons extra-virgin olive oil

1 pound fideos (or substitute angel hair pasta, broken into 2-inch pieces)

8 cups Fish Stock (recipe follows)

Mallorcan (or Maldon) sea salt and freshly ground black pepper

1 pound cleaned calamari, cut into ½-inch pieces, preferably with its ink

Heat ¼ cup of the olive oil in a large sauté pan over medium heat. Add the *fideos* and cook, stirring constantly, until well browned, 8 to 10 minutes. Add 2 cups of the fish stock and bring to a boil. Season with salt and pepper to taste. Cook the *fideos* until al dente, adding the remaining stock a cup at a time and simmering until it is almost completely absorbed after each addition. The *fideos* should be soft but not mushy.

Add the calamari, with its ink if you have it, and cook for 1 minute, or until tender. Remove from the heat, stir in the remaining 2 tablespoons oil, and serve.

fish stock   MAKES ABOUT 4 QUARTS

3 pounds fish scraps from non-oily fish (such as heads and tails from rockfish)

1 onion, coarsely chopped

2 stalks celery, coarsely chopped

2 bay leaves

1 teaspoon black peppercorns

Put everything in a large stockpot, cover with cold water, and bring just to a simmer. Skim off the foam, reduce the heat slightly, and simmer gently, uncovered, for 25 minutes. Strain the stock through a fine sieve.

MENORCA

For a great day trip, Claudia and I jump on a plane to make the twenty-minute trip to neighboring Menorca, a windswept, somewhat distant version of Mallorca. Menorca's not nearly as mountainous as Mallorca, there are just some little hills. It has refused development and remains wonderfully untouched. We meet two fishermen, Paco and Aleix, who take us on their boat, show us how to make a tasty lobster stew, sing us old songs, and drink the most junipery gin, a local specialty, I've ever tasted. I take a few sips in an effort to be good company, but it really doesn't go down too easily at ten a.m. I guess I will never make it as a Menorcan fisherman. . . .

We are ferried out from the dock by Paco, who is either the happiest, most song-filled dude I have ever met or a walking ad for life in Menorca, or both. We get to the lobster boat, though I should really say "fishing boat," because we find out that lobster season is spring and summer and that collection of these Mediterranean sweets is strictly prohibited the rest of the year. So these fellows fish for finfish for six months of the year, and lobsters when the running is good. And for good reason: they can get 100 Euros a kilo from the local restaurants for the lobsters, so even a couple or three a day is a good living. We see a veritable array of high-end Mediterranean fish, including porgy, branzino, scorpion fish, black bass, and something that looks a bit like pompano, and then the lobsters—two of about one and a quarter pounds each and a champion of about three pounds—all the while listening to these two old pals cracking jokes, singing, and celebrating life in general. Their enthusiasm is infectious, and as we head in to the dock to observe the making of the famous *caldereta de langosta*, or fisherman's lobster stew, I feel confident we will have a good lunch.

We set up a fire on the shore and start to put together the stew. There's a little too much wind, so it goes more slowly than Aleix would like, but we persevere, with gin, hard work, and half a wheel of the local Maó cheese to tide us over. We make a quick little add-on sauce with the lobster roe, raw garlic, and Spanish brandy that frightens me at first, but it is stirred into the hot stew, so it loses its hot raw garlic flavor and, actually, the brandy gives the *caldereta* heft. The lobster is exquisite, and I am more sure than ever that I prefer this kind of lobster to the Maine lobsters back at home. Claudia agrees with me that Gwyneth would truly love this dish and these folks, but sadly, she does not arrive until tomorrow.

fisherman's
LOBSTER STEW

As is true of any traditional local dish, every cook makes this stew differently. In fact, our two fishermen, Paco and Aleix, disputed how long things should cook and in what order. The secret to the dish is in the sauce, and it's all about reserving the roe from the lobster, which is mixed with punchy garlic, bright parsley, and a swig of brandy.

SERVES 6

Two 1½-pound female Menorcan lobsters (or Caribbean or Maine lobsters)

½ cup extra-virgin olive oil

1 large Spanish onion, cut into ¼-inch dice

2 plum tomatoes, coarsely chopped

2 cubanelle peppers, coarsely chopped

4 garlic cloves, thinly sliced

Sea salt and freshly ground black pepper

1 bunch Italian parsley, leaves removed and finely chopped

¼ cup brandy

To kill the lobsters, hold each one firmly on a cutting board with its head toward you, plunge a sharp heavy knife into the center of the head, and quickly bring the knife down to the board, splitting the front of the lobster in half; turn it around and cut it completely in half. Pull off the tails, and then pull off the claws if using Maine lobsters. Slice the tails into ½-inch medallions, cutting through the natural segments in the shells. Remove the roe from the bodies and reserve; remove and discard the head sacs and tomalley.

Heat 6 tablespoons of the olive oil in a paella pan or a large sauté pan over high heat. Add the lobster heads, claws if you have them, and tail pieces and sauté for 1 minute, or until they turn red. Transfer the heads (and claws) to one bowl and the tail pieces to another. Add the onion, tomatoes, peppers, and half the garlic to the pan and cook until softened, 8 to 10 minutes. Add 8 cups water, bring to a boil, and season with salt and pepper. Add the lobster heads (and claws) and simmer for 10 minutes. Add the tail pieces and cook for 3 to 5 minutes, until opaque throughout. Remove the stew from the heat and let rest while you make the sauce.

Combine the reserved roe, the remaining 2 tablespoons oil, the remaining garlic, the parsley, and brandy in a mortar and mash to a loose paste with the pestle. Add to the stew and stir well, then check for seasoning and serve.

CAN JOAN DE S'AIGO

We fly back to Mallorca that night, and early the next morning, I take Claudia to Can Joan de S'aigo because, as she herself says, she gets cranky in the morning if she doesn't eat. It's the best place in town to carbo-load before a day of golf, and it's especially important to try their famed *ensaimadas*, flaky pastries with different fillings.

The place has been around since 1700, but it didn't start out as a pastry and coffee shop. In fact, the original owners (currently the ninth generation of the same family runs the shop) went up in the Mallorcan mountains to collect and pack ice, and the store sold glasses of water with ice—which was an ultimate luxury at the time. Around the beginning of the twentieth century, they started to make ice creams in a whole variety of flavors. From ice to ice cream and then from ice cream to pastry, Can Joan de S'aigo has always been a place to quench your thirst or satisfy your sweet tooth.

I eat a large breakfast before golfing, so that I don't have to stop for a silly thing like lunch. Claudia impressively keeps up with me. We start with strong coffees and *ensaimadas*. The most interesting one is filled with *sobrasada* (a soft, rich pork sausage) and *membrillo* (quince paste). It has a surprisingly perfect balance of salty, savory, porky meat and sugary pastry. Then we take forkfuls of the *tarta de almendras* (almond cake). During February, the white flowers on the almond trees bloom and when the blossoms fall off, the whole island looks as if it's been snowed on.

By now our table, covered with plates of pastries, is quite a sight. We continue to sample. An empanada with lamb is intensely savory, and a pastry stuffed with spaghetti squash, raisins, and cinnamon prompts Claudia to say that she tastes Christmas. We move on to a few *cocas* (basically small Spanish pizzas). One with Swiss chard, anchovies, and a slice of tomato is satisfying in a vegetal way; another has peppers and onions cooked to such sweet perfection that they almost taste of candy. As our waiter clears our plates, we're left with a mere shadow of our initial appetites.

But we're not finished yet! It's time for dessert. Tall glasses filled with *helado* (ice cream) arrive. The flavors are big and round: the almond tastes of Mallorca, the hazelnut is rich and nutty, the chocolate a hit, the meringue a floaty dream, and the strawberry—its color alone is enough to make me dream a hallucination of fruit! It's full of flavor, a bright, clean strawberry punch. All the ice creams have the texture of ripe peaches, not the soft, almost taffy-like pull of gelato—you take a bite, and soon your spoonful vanishes, a melting moment of intense flavor.

I think it's no coincidence that I happened to be wearing my Wheaties T-shirt. Claudia and I have conquered a *desayuno de los campeones* (breakfast of champions).

CLAUDIA: I don't drink coffee, but I order it anyway. Mario thinks I'm nuts, but I adore the smell and enjoy holding the hot cup in my hands.

¿QUÉ es?

BENJAMÍN: We see *benjamín* listed on the drinks menu at Can Joan de S'aigo. We find out that a *benjamín* is a small bottle of cava, a single serving. Apparently in local slang the *benjamín* of the family is the smallest child, hence the smallest bottle. Great for sipping with breakfast.

The chef here, Joan Olives i Mercadal, is to be trusted. And his restaurant, with walls made of wine crates, is not to be missed. It works as follows: no menu, no pretense—the chef just sits down with you and tells you what's available, asks you what you like, and all of a sudden your dialogue turns into a wonderful, memorable meal. Importantly, the chef values wine—he views it not as an extra element to the meal, but as one of the core essentials.

Our first course consists of line-caught calamari that's been cooked on a smoking-hot *plancha*. The ink is emulsified with olive oil to form a sauce. The wine, a white from northern Mallorca, is a thoughtful marriage, and Claudia and I enter into squid bliss. I notice some mysterious acidity in the dish that makes it just delicious—perhaps a splash of vinegar, a squeeze of lemon? Joan tells us he hasn't added any acid and that the fresh, clean taste comes from cooking the calamari without oil—it's thrown on the *plancha* in its naked state, and heat is the only thing that touches it. Generally there's a faint fattiness to squid, not quite like butter, but the same resounding mouthfeel as butter. Here the squid is unadulterated and light. Totally wonderful.

Next come some of the greatest beans of my life, and I'm a bean dude (not the way Mark's a bean dude—I'm more of a young whippersnapper of a bean dude). The beans, *habas* (dried fava beans), are cooked in sausage fat and served with two types of sausage, *butifarra* and a kind of *sobrasada/morcilla* cross, but without the *pimentón*. When the chef presents the dish, I tell him that he's singing my song. The beans look as if they might be dry, but they're absolutely not—the wrinkly skin gives way to a creamy, succulent interior. To make the experience that much greater, we drink a wonderful wine that's full of acid and fruit that balances the deepness of the beans and sausage. It's a *tinto* made with a grape called Manto Negro, and it's a local wine.

Our third dish is an *arroz* with red mullet, one of my two favorite fish from the Mediterranean (the other is scorpion fish), because it has the nice rich taste of where you are. The dish is especially flavorful because it's made with a strong fish stock. It's served in a small paella pan set on top of a wooden board. The rice at the bottom of the pan is crispy, and Joan scoops up our servings from the bottom, incorporating the crispy bits with the softer rice in the middle. The wonderful red color comes from the skin of a particular type of dried pepper that fisherman have always traditionally taken with them on their boats to flavor their dishes. It seems a bit crazy to serve this dish with red wine, but it actually works and is, in fact, just right.

The fourth dish is *pescado* (fish) cooked inside of *coca*, the pizzalike bread we ate for

Our first course consists of line-caught calamari that's been cooked on a smoking-hot *plancha*. The ink is emulsified with olive oil to form a sauce. Claudia and I enter into squid bliss.

breakfast. It arrives in a rectangular dish and looks almost like a potpie. The top is covered with a thin layer of the bread dough, which we must cut through to release the magnificent fragrance. It's kind of like fish cooked in parchment paper, but in this case you can eat both the contents and the package. Inside, we find moist hake with fat olives, fennel, and a bit of tomato. We stick with the same red wine and, again, it's surprisingly on point.

To end with, a dessert that looks at first like lemon meringue pie. The bottom is a thick layer of almond cake and the top is an airy pile of meringue. In between is a creamy layer of egg yolks cooked with sugar, like a dense zabaglione. There's also a streak of strawberry puree on the plate—Joan says it's a stripe from the twenty-first century. The cake is served with a strong, sweet Moscatel from late-harvest grapes, and both the flavor and fragrance put us into a sweet, peaceful state.

I have to give it to her—Claudia picked a pretty great place for lunch and, although it's hard for me to admit, she actually drove pretty well.

¿QUÉ es? **SOBRASADA**: *Sobrasada* is one of Mallorca's most famous foods. A soft, almost spreadable sausage made from pork, *pimentón*, and a bit of pork fat, it's rich and flavorful, assertive and unmistakable. You find it all over the island—on slices of bread, served as a tapa, and even in sweet pastries (which qualifies the island as Batali paradise).

· CATHEDRAL ·

LA SEU

· MALLORCA ·

The Cathedral of Palma, called La Seu, is literally built up to the waterfront, the only church in Europe so constructed. Built on the site of a Moorish mosque, it was begun under James I in 1230 and completed almost four hundred years later, in 1601. Legend has it that in 1229, the royal fleet was struck by a heavy storm when sailing to Mallorca, and James, certain that he was going to perish, prayed to the Virgin Mary to save him. When he survived, he determined to build a cathedral in her honor, and construction was begun on the magnificent church the following year. A masterpiece of Gothic architecture, it features looming bell towers, a magnificent rose window, and a spectacular and imposing limestone façade that looms over the city's walls, a reminder of the Christian conquest to all who sailed into port. Gaudí added a delicate and partly unfinished touch between 1904 and 1914: a wrought-iron canopy, draped with colored Christmas lights, over the main altar that is both frightening and inviting. Contemporary artist Miquel Barceló's ceramic mural in the Chapel of St. Peter, a bizarre and beautiful ode to life, fish, and bread, has inspired controversy over both its art and its expense. The place is totally cool and, needless to say, one of my favorite cathedrals in all of Spain.

 ¿QUÉ es? **MAÓ**: Maó, aka Mahón, is a cows'-milk cheese made in the Balearics, and it's worth seeking out. It's strong but not too assertive, firm but not hard, and it's delicious on a piece of good bread, alongside a glass of wine, or simply in thick slices straight from the wheel. Apparently in Menorca they usually eat it with a highball of gin and sour lemon juice—not my recommendation, but it's always worth knowing tradition.

You can't come to Mallorca without having *ensaimada*, and you haven't had *ensaimada* until you've had Miguel Pujol's. An *ensaimada* is a round pastry made from sweet dough that's coiled into a distinctive spiral. The name comes from the word *saim*, the Catalan term for "lard." It makes sense, since there's an absurdly fabulous amount of lard inside—I knew there was a reason I was drawn to this place.

Miguel is a sweet man and a generous teacher in the style of a Zen master. He learned how to prepare *ensaimada* in the classic tradition of apprenticeship, and he worked with a *maestro*. He tells a story of commitment, of when he was younger and wanted to rush to a party, and therefore rush the *ensaimada*, but his teacher made him stay and do it correctly. Miguel is sixty years old and will be forced to retire in five years. Where's the Board of Mallorcan Tourism and Irreplaceableness when you need it? He kindly offered to teach Claudia and me how to make *ensaimadas* in his bakery and, while we won't be continuing the tradition in Mallorca, we can properly acknowledge it here.

A note about the bakery: its oven has been around since 1565 and Miguel's family started making *ensaimadas* in 1914. He has been here for forty-four years and works every day on a wooden board that he says would sink in a second if it were thrown into the ocean since it's so saturated with olive oil and lard.

The dough is made from grease and flour and sugar, plus a few eggs and some *masa madre*, or mother dough (like a sourdough starter). Miguel, his delicate hands covered in oil and his shoes caked in flour, begins to translate cultural history through his craft; he is wise and thoughtful, kind and engaging. He pours in a bit of olive oil only at the very end of mixing to refine the dough. It's kneaded a bit and then left to rest. While it's resting, he offers us a glass of *cava*. While we're sipping, Miguel explains the history of *ensaimadas*, a history of scarcity and preservation. He explains that before there was refrigeration, and ice was still a luxury, lard was one of the most economical ways of storing and preserving foods, among them eggs. Miguel says an egg could stay fresh under lard's protection for months! So, as the story goes, eventually the eggs and lard were combined with flour and a yeast starter made from the fermentation power of a rotting tomato, and the first *ensaimada* was coiled.

The rested dough has remarkable elasticity, like a strudel dough, and its resilience is amazing. I ask Miguel why it doesn't tear, and he replies, nonchalantly, "Because it's well made." He spreads a handful of lard over the dough with his fingers. I admire his economy, seeing that he wastes not a spoonful of lard. He tops the dough with "angel's hair" spaghetti squash that's been cooked down with sugar, cinnamon, and lemon zest, then rolls up the pastry tightly and dances it into a spiral. He puts it into onto an old dark pan and leaves it to rest overnight.

Miguel retrieves an *ensaimada* dough he prepared the day before and bakes it in the vintage-1565 oven for 15 minutes (although, as we soon find out, 15 minutes in Mallorca is more like 30). The room smells of sugar, fat, and fire. Miguel shakes powdered sugar on top of the *ensaimada* like snow and hands us pieces of crispy-on-the outside, soft-on-the-inside deliciousness. In one bite, we experience the history of the recipe and the age of the oven. It is an excellent example of how food is an amazing traveler through cultures, perhaps the best single vehicle to explain societal change at the very primary level. I am humbled in the presence of the master. Miguel takes a bite and says, softly, "*dulce.*" Sweet indeed.

> **GWYNETH**: What other gastronomic trouble can we get into today?

Although I didn't make it to a golf course with Claudia, I'm convinced that Gwyneth will join me. I invite her to my room for breakfast and to practice a few swings. As it goes, that's the only golf I end up playing in Mallorca—but when you're eating *jamón* for breakfast and then spending the day with Gwyneth, it's difficult to complain.

We get into a conversation about high school jobs, and she tells me she was once a reservationist at the famous Santa Monica airport restaurant D–3, during her summer break. She worked in a basement room that didn't have windows and whose walls were lined with Metro shelving stacked with toilet paper. She'd chain-smoke and overbook the restaurant, because she felt bad saying no to people.

We move on from bad jobs to wonderful kids. Her children are, in her words, "divine." I tell her it's the juiciest thing, having kids, better than lasagne. She can't stand this comparison because she hates lasagne—which shocks me. Hate lasagne? Soon we realize that she just hasn't had great lasagne. We'll fix that after the road trip.

GRILLING BY THE SEA

Claudia spends the day recovering from all of our eating and Gwyneth and I set up a grill under an olive tree on the wild Mallorcan coast. We have a bounty of local foods—fish, sausages, beautiful vegetables, strong olive oil, and sea salt. Our friend Guillermo Méndez, who runs El Olivo, the restaurant at our hotel, joins us. When I explain to him that Gwyneth doesn't eat meat and will be forgoing the sausage, he responds that not eating meat is like a painter leaving red out of his painting. I like this man.

We grill our lunch and eat it overlooking the sea. The water is all shades of blue and green and teal, and the waves crash in loud white bursts. This is definitely the best way to eat Mallorcan food—outside, by the water, with friends. It's the best table in the house (even if it is the only table in the house).

MARIO: Everything that grows here seems blessed.

RECIPE

Mallorcan
MIXED GRILL

Simple and unbeatable. A lesson in great ingredients.

SERVES 4

1 large Mallorcan lobster
   (or Caribbean or
   Maine lobster)
A few whole mackerel,
   cleaned and scaled
1 rouget, cleaned and scaled
12 large head-on shrimp
   in the shell
Extra-virgin olive oil
Mallorcan or Maldon sea salt

To kill the lobster, hold it firmly on a cutting board with its head toward you, plunge a sharp heavy knife into the center of the head, and quickly bring the knife down to the board, splitting the front of the lobster in half; turn it around and cut it completely in half.

Rub the lobster, fish, and shrimp with olive oil and season with salt (including the cavities of the fish). Put over a hot grill fire (start the lobster shell side down) and cook the shrimp for about 2 minutes, the lobster, mackerel, and rouget for 4 to 5 minutes, or until the flesh is starting to become opaque; don't give in to the temptation to flip too soon. Use a spatula to gently turn the shrimp, and then the lobster and fish, and cook for a few more minutes more, until just cooked through. Transfer to a platter, sprinkle with salt and olive oil, and dig in.

HOW DO YOU
TAKE YOUR COFFEE

GWYNETH:

With
HOT SOY MILK.

MARIO:

CORTADO
(a small strong coffee with a tiny bit of milk)
WITH HALF A SUGAR.

CLAUDIA:

I JUST LIKE THE SMELL.

MARK:

DEPENDS ON MY MOOD
and the time of day.

WHAT WE'RE LOOKING FORWARD TO

I'm a bit sad I never made it to a golf course, but it's
hard to complain about the incredible time we had in
Mallorca and Menorca. Next we're jetting to Valencia,
because it wouldn't be Spain without true paella.

12

From VALENCIA to MADRID

WHERE WE'RE GOING

Behold the land of oranges and paella! We couldn't be happier to be going to Valencia. Gwyneth and I head toward the rice fields to meet Manuelo, who is the Ultimate Paella Iron Chef. Mark and Claudia opt for the urban life and drive around to check out Calatrava's incredible buildings (this is, after all, Calatrava's hometown).

WHAT WE'RE EATING

VALENCIA

Valencia was established as a Roman city on the Turia River in the late second century BC. It was later sacked and taken by the Visigoths, and then by the Moors, who took over the city without resistance in the early eighth century, along with the rest of the Iberian Peninsula. The beautifully maintained architectural splendor created under Moorish rule was allowed to survive as a base for James I after his conquest of the city in 1238 in the name of the crown of Aragon. The city's position on the coast assured Valencia of both wealth and influence. The first printing press in Spain was here and the first Spanish Bible was printed here. Home to modern architect rock star Santiago Calatrava, twenty-first century Valencia is a virtual modern paradise, with Calatrava's vast urban complex, The City of Arts and Science, as its flagship.

· RESTAURANT ·

CASA MONTAÑA

· VALENCIA ·

Gwyneth, Claudia, Mark, and I all get together at Casa Montaña, an old-fashioned tapas bar in the center of Valencia. It's fun for all four us to be together again, and we celebrate with a lot of food and a lot of wine.

OUR MENU at CASA MONTAÑA

PATATAS BRAVAS *(made with hand-selected potatoes)*

HABAS *(large brown beans with ham)*

FABAS *(small green beans dressed with ham, lemon, and orange)*

Preserved **BERBERECHOS** *(Galician clams)*

Steamed **FRESH BERBERECHOS** *(eaten with a toast to the Galician mariscadoras)*

TOMATOES *with sea salt and olive oil*

JAMÓN

PIQUILLO PEPPERS *stuffed with tuna in béchamel*

BRANDADE *on toasts*

Baby **ARTICHOKE HEARTS**

SEAWEED *with soft scrambled eggs*

Grilled **SARDINES**

Fried **ANCHOVIES**

CALAMARI a la plancha

BOQUERONES *(anchovies marinated in vinegar)*

CHORIZO

TERNERA CECINA *(dried veal) with lemon and olive oil*

Sliced **VALENCIA ORANGES**

Chocolate **TRUFFLES**

RUSSIAN CAKE

MUCHO VINO *y poca agua (a lot of wine and a little water)*

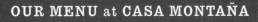

CHATTER

MARK: Can I have a glass of white wine? I can't start with red wine.

MARIO: Yeah, starting with red wine is like taking a sleeping pill before going to a museum.

MARK: These beans are delicious. What do they call them?

MARIO: *Habas.*

MARK: What does that mean?

MARIO: Beans.

MARIO: Here, try some of these canned *berberechos.*

GWYNETH: I thought the can was just conceptual plating.

MARIO: No! Canned seafood in Spain is special stuff—prized.

GWYNETH: Strange. Normally if I was offered a can of clams, I would say, "No."

MARK: I haven't had ham this good in . . .

MARIO: A day!

MARK: Funny. Throughout this entire road trip, no one has been able to seduce Gwyneth into eating *jamón.*

MARK: What do you call a doggy bag in Spanish?

MARIO: *¿Una bolsa de perros?*

CLAUDIA: I love when they wrap it like a swan!

MARIO: That's only in movies.

CLAUDIA: No it's not!

MARIO: I guess I finish my food most of the time.

GWYNETH: Mark came to visit me in New York. I was so excited for "Mark Bittman" to cook in my kitchen!

MARIO: What did he make?

GWYNETH: He boiled some spaghetti and stirred it with olive oil.

MARK: Hey! It was good!

MARK: Claudia has tried a lot of new things on this trip.

CLAUDIA: Yes! I've had brains, shrimp heads, and oysters, and in Mallorca I ate a massacre of an animal—the heart, the liver!

GWYNETH: And I just ate beans that were cooked with pork!

MARIO: You're living on the edge!

MARK: But neither of you women ate the *percebes.*

GWYNETH: I think there should be a law that if something's that ugly, you don't have to eat it.

MARK: I've eaten uglier things.

MARIO: I find them quite attractive.

GWYNETH: You guys have this thing about eating the weirdest food—I think it's some sort of macho thing.

MARK: No it's not!

MARIO: I think I'm macho.

grilled
SARDINES

These came in especially handy for Gwyneth when our table was covered with plates of all kinds of pork. It's important to keep everyone happy!

SERVES 4

1 pound sardines, cleaned
and scaled

Extra-virgin olive oil

Coarse sea salt

1 lemon, preferably from
Valencia, cut into
4 or 8 wedges

Rub the sardines with just enough oil to make them slick, and sprinkle with salt. Put over a hot grill fire and cook until well marked with grill marks, 3 to 4 minutes; when the sardines are ready to be turned, they will release easily from the grill. Using a spatula, carefully turn and cook for 3 more minutes, or until just opaque throughout. Transfer to a platter, sprinkle with salt, and drizzle with a little more olive oil. Serve with the lemon wedges.

HABAS GIGANTES

These were especially loved by Mark, who goes wild for beans of any kind.
Slightly porky and smoky, they were great for nibbling while nursing our vino.

SERVES 6

1 pound dried peeled fava beans,
    soaked overnight in water
    to cover

¼ cup extra-virgin olive oil

A 2-ounce chunk of slab bacon

A 2-ounce piece of *jamón serrano*,
    from the shank (you can
    substitute prosciutto)

2 ounces *butifarra* or other
    pork sausage

1 Spanish onion, cut into
    ¼-inch dice

½ cup dry red wine

Coarse sea salt

Drain the beans. Put them in a large pot, add water to cover by 2 inches, and bring to a boil. Reduce the heat and simmer until barely tender, about 1½ hours; add water if necessary to keep the beans covered. Drain.

Combine the olive oil, meats, and onion in a large pot and cook over medium heat, stirring, until the meats are browned and the onion is soft, about 10 minutes. Add the beans, wine, and enough water to cover and bring to a simmer. Reduce the heat slightly and simmer gently for 30 minutes, or until the beans are very tender. Remove from the heat, remove the meats from the pot, and let cool slightly.

Slice the bacon and ham, and cut the sausages into 1-inch pieces. Return to the beans, stir to mix, and season with salt. Serve hot.

NARANJA: *Naranja* is the Spanish word for orange. Valencia is famous for its oranges, and they're super flavorful and abundant. You see orange trees all over the place—in the city's parks, beside the highways, in every backyard. They're a great way to start the morning and to end a meal. When the orange trees blossom in the late spring around Holy Week, the whole town is high on their fragrant essence.

Santiago Calatrava, the world-renowned architect and sculptor, was born in Valencia. No surprise that some of his most famous buildings can be found in his hometown. The eastern part of the city is dominated by his Ciudad de las Artes y las Ciencias, The City of Arts and Sciences, consisting of five buildings: El Palacio de las Artes Reina Sofía (an opera house), L'Hemiesféric (a planetarium), L'Umbracle (a walkway and garden), El Museo de las Ciencias (a science museum), and L'Oceanográfic (an oceanographic park). The area was previously a dry riverbed, but Calatrava's structures are very water dominated. In fact, there are streams and pools throughout the entire "city," and the opera house looks like an abstract fish. Calatrava's work is unabashedly skeletal. His buildings often exhibit their internal structure, and these structures seem to be based on the skeletal arrangement of bones. His style seems particularly emblematic of contemporary Spain—influenced by nature but determined to push forward in new directions. Without a doubt, his buildings are thrilling.

Manuelo Baixauli, the paella Zen master, is a quiet, focused man. He has meaty asbestos hands, he waddles more than walks, and he is wearing worn black corduroy pants and a newsboy cap. He's the kind of cook you really have to watch, because he won't tell you much—his techniques are conveyed through his movements. Although he tells me that the most traditional paella is made with rabbit, duck, and other meats, he agrees to show us how to make a seafood paella as a gesture towards Gwyneth, our non–meat eater.

Ideally paella should be made outside on a wood fire—this gives it the requisite smoke for the best texture and flavor. Manuelo builds his fire with wood from orange trees. He places a large paella pan on an iron stand over the fire and pours in a healthy dose of olive oil. He adds some beautiful *cigalas* (basically large scampi), which he cooks for a short while and then removes. Then come onions, pureed tomatoes, saffron, cuttlefish, and sweet *pimentón*. The mix is an amazing orange-red color and its smell is more than a promise, it is a guarantee. Cue the rich fish broth and chunks of monkfish. Then, after the excitement of a rolling boil, Manuelo adds the most wonderful Valencian bomba rice, stirring to distribute it evenly. He rests a few clams on top and returns the *cigalas* to the party. He lets it all cook, without stirring, until it reaches what I might have

previously thought of as burning, or at least sticking badly. Manuelo knows when it's done just by the sound, the smell, and the sight—no touching or tasting, as I'm used to. He fashions two pot holders out of newspaper, he and I each take a handle, and we march the paella, a bit triumphantly, to the table.

Gwyneth and I sit down with Manuelo, and Rafa, who owns La Matandeta, joins us with his wife and grandson. We ignore our plates and eat straight from the pan, squeezing a bit of fresh lemon onto each spoonful. Manuelo assures us that the paella is the perfect texture, because when he turns his spoon upside down, the paella stays put—it's sticky enough to stay solid but not dense enough to weigh itself down. He asks if I like it and I tell him, "No, I love it." You can taste the fire and smoke—the paella tastes of where it was made, how it was tranformed from raw ingredient to final product. And, just like Italians treat pasta, Spaniards respect rice and make it the star of their dishes. The other ingredients—the spices, the seafood—act almost like a dressing, a condiment. The rice is enhanced—not masked. Its greatness is majestically celebrated.

I ask Manuelo what he thinks of paellas from other parts of Spain. "They're not paella," he responds. It seems that paella is loyal to its birthplace—food can transcend, but authenticity isn't so mobile.

PAELLA

It's difficult to duplicate the experience of cooking paella with Manuelo outdoors in Valencia over burning embers of wood from orange trees, but you could do it on a grill on high heat. Most important, buy a proper pan (available at www.latienda.com), cook it a little longer than you think, and DON'T STIR! If you are cooking it indoors on the stove, be generous with the super-smoky pimentón since it will provide the requisite almost-but-not-quite-burned flavor. In Spain, the almost-burned, slightly sticky, crunchy crust that forms on the bottom of the paella pan, called soccarat, is the most coveted part of the dish. Some cooks stir the soccarat into the rest of the paella when serving, others save it for the end.

SERVES 6

½ cup extra-virgin olive oil

6 large scampi or Dublin Bay
    prawns in the shell

1 medium Spanish onion,
    cut into ¼-inch dice

½ cup pureed ripe tomatoes

1 teaspoon kosher salt,
    or to taste

1 teaspoon saffron threads

1 tablespoon sweet pimentón
    (Spanish smoked paprika)

1 pound cleaned cuttlefish
    (or substitute calamari),
    cut into 1-inch pieces

2 quarts Fish Stock (page 283)

2 cups bomba or other
    short-grain rice

1 pound monkfish tail, cleaned
    and cut into ½-inch cubes

1 pound Manila clams, scrubbed

Heat a 14- to 18-inch paella pan over medium-high heat. Add the oil and heat until smoking. Add the scampi and cook until golden brown on both sides, about 3 minutes per side. Transfer to a plate and set aside. Add the onion to the pan and cook until soft, about 8 minutes. Add the tomato puree, stirring it into the onions, and cook for 3 minutes. Add the salt, saffron, pimentón, and cuttlefish and cook, stirring, for 5 minutes, or until the cuttlefish firms up slightly. Add the stock, bring to a boil, and cook for 5 minutes. Add the rice and stir well to distribute it evenly. Add the monkfish and clams, arranging them nicely, bring the stock back to a boil, and cook, without stirring, for 10 minutes. Add the scampi, taste for salt, and cook, again without stirring, for 10 to 15 more minutes, or until the liquid is almost completely absorbed and the pan starts to make a crackling noise (don't worry, this is what you want). Remove from the heat and let rest for 10 minutes before serving.

Because we were so excited to get the trip started, we barely saw Madrid when we first flew into the city and then we were anxious to get to Toledo and beyond. Well, we came to our senses and realized we had to spend a bit more time in the capital. We also convinced our good friend, famed chef-cum-artist Ferran Adrià, to come meet us. Definitely a memorable time.

LUNCH WITH FERRAN

Ferran Adrià is, without exaggeration, the most famous chef in the world. He started out as a restaurant dishwasher in 1980, cooked in the military, and then, at the age of twenty-three, became the head chef at El Bulli in Roses, at the time a good but hardly exceptional restaurant. Over the last nearly twenty-five years, he has transformed it into a pilgrimage site. He's not so much a cook as he is an artist, a postmodern deconstructionist obsessed with the way food provokes culture and vice versa. His goal is not to just feed you, but also to offer an intellectual and emotional experience. When eating Ferran's food, you cannot not think. He forces you to confront your ideas of normalcy and artistry, to compound your notion of consumption, and to complicate your understanding of art.

Because El Bulli is open only from April through October, we couldn't meet with Ferran on his home turf, but we were lucky enough to be invited to La Terraza del Casino, the Madrid restaurant where his disciple, Paco Roncero, cooks Ferran-directed food. There Ferran joined us for a memorable lunch.

We begin with a "cocktail"—as if it were that simple! The cocktail, a variation on the Brazilian caipirinha, consists of fresh lime juice, cachaça (Brazilian sugarcane liquor), and, of course, liquid nitrogen. The three are mixed together in a stainless steel bowl and then the frozen mass, very much like a sorbet, is scooped into hollowed-out lime shells. It looks like a green egg overflowing with meringue, but it's frozen alcohol! It's a solid cocktail! It's amazing, to say the least.

We move onto a discussion about the kitchen as a multidisciplinary arena, revolving around health, anthropology, economics, even religion. Ferran points out that food is the most important thing—without it, he says, you will die. Hard to argue with that, but it becomes increasingly clear that beyond that, he thinks about food from a perspective very different from that of most people. It's not about instant gratification, it's not really about nourishment; rather, he thinks about food in terms of theory rather than necessity. Food is a means for Ferran to express his understanding of—and his complications with—the ways of the world. Food is a means for him to offer digestible articulations of intricate thought processes.

Then our next course arrives, a mandarin orange bonbon that has the thinnest possible shell and tastes and feels like butterfat. It's surprising and, in one small bite, gone. It's followed by what appears to be a gigantic cigarette ash: it's actually a black sesame and miso biscuit. Mark says it looks like lava. I eat it in two bites and smile.

Our next course is a thinner-than-thin variation on a Mexican tortilla that tastes like a *fricco* from Friuli but is in fact made of corn with a generous shaving of the year's last truffles. We begin to realize that all the contemporary dishes we've recently eaten around the world—the foams and deconstructed plates, the too-sweet entrées and overly salty desserts—are all watered-down derivatives of the original, Ferran's authentic experiments and creations. Ferran begins to pontificate about water. He makes us all smell our glasses of water, consider the water, reflect on it, and then, a bit nervously, sip it. With Ferran you always see things differently. You taste and understand them in new ways.

Next we have a mushroom sandwich that is so thin we are asked to hold onto it tightly for fear it may fly off in the wind. It consists of a thin, crispy exterior bread made with cheese instead of flour (OK, like there is some flour in it) with meltingly soft mushrooms and cheese inside. This is followed by a sort of croquette filled with baby salmon roe. A bit of roe falls into my palm and before I can retrieve it, Gwyneth grabs my hand and licks it off. It's that good.

When our next course, I think we're up to six, arrives, Ferran picks up his plate and sniffs it. "You smell wine, why not food?" We taste, and soon "oh-my-God's" and mm's and aah's erupt. The dish is, per Ferran's description, "the best gnocchi you've ever had." Could be. It is followed by a plate of "beans"— yeah, right. These beans are the "essence of beans in bean essence skin." Basically, a highly concentrated, incredibly flavorful puree of beans is combined with a bit of sodium algenate and then dipped into a water-and–calcium chloride solution that "sets" the outside, forming a thin, strong spherical shell.

Our next and final savory course consists of lobster with olive oil soup and dots of flavorful, citrusy purees around the plate's rim. Ferran explains the importance of reading a plate, taking it in. Gwyneth asks him to describe the process, and he refuses: he says either you can read it or you can't. It's not something to be learned. Well, okay. Mark and I both go for the top left corner of our plates—we are, after all, reading. This first bite is the blue flower from the borage plant. We continue around the top of the plate, working our way down the page.

For dessert, we have olive oil ravioli with chocolate powder and passion fruit. Gwyneth wipes the last bit of sweet from her plate and tells Ferran that she thought her dinner at Inopia, run by Ferran's brother in Barcelona, was the best meal she had in Spain, but now she's not sure. Ferran points out that Paco cooked this meal, not him. Gwyneth still hasn't been to El Bulli. She still hasn't had the best meal in Spain.

 ¿QUÉ es? **LIQUID NITROGEN**: Ferran often employs liquid nitrogen in his cooking, but he explains that it's "just a tool, like anything else." In a way, it makes sense—like fire or acid, applying liquid nitrogen to food manipulates it, transforming it from one state to another. Liquid nitrogen is pure nitrogen in a liquid state, and it boils at minus 321°F. Pretty cold. It freezes things on contact. To demonstrate liquid nitrogen's abilities, Ferran had Paco dip a rose into it, and when it emerged, Gwyneth gently flicked it with her fingers. We were surrounded by shattered petals.

EL PRADO WITH FERRAN

We visit the Prado, Madrid's world-renowned museum, with Ferran. What better setting to discuss the relationship between food and art? It's a complicated relationship and, as we know, Ferran is a complicated man.

First we have to define art, the larger umbrella under which we have to figure out where food falls. Ferran considers the issue, then reaches into my bag and pulls out my iPod. He talks about twenty-first-century design, about the intelligence behind creation. "If you're able to move consciousness forward, it's art," Ferran says. Even Mark agrees that this is a good definition.

Ferran then attempts to locate food within the sphere of art. It's difficult because of food's ephemeral nature. To explain the concept, he points to the painting that's hanging behind us. It's, of course, virtually the same now as when the painter put down his brush. A plate of food, though, can only last so long, it doesn't have the same permanence. One of the important consequences of food's short life span is its reliance on cultural memory. We must remember how the food tasted, where it was made, whose hands carried it. The history of food, in other words, relies on our memory of it, on our preservation of its emotional and cultural significance.

So, food doesn't have the permanence of traditional forms of visual art, doesn't have the longevity. But does that mean it isn't art? Mark argues that food is like a piece of music—you can make it over and over again, both duplicate and reinvent it. A good point. But Ferran doesn't really buy it, because the products are alive and therefore always changing. You can never eat the same dish twice. It doesn't exist in replication.

So, food is short-lived and always changing. But can't it be art? Ferran answers with the bold statement that "If you don't see this painting, you won't die. If you don't eat, you'll die." True enough. But it still doesn't really answer the question. I ask him if a plate of spaghetti can ever be art. Before he answers, Gwyneth quickly interjects, "It is in my world." Her enthusiasm reflects the energy and passion spurred by food, even the mere thought of food. Kind of like art, no?

It doesn't look as if we're going to get an easy explanation of the relationship between art and food. But Ferran has encouraged Spain and, ultimately, the world to break boundaries in the perception of food. To incorporate provocation, reflection, and humor on the plate. I'd say that's changing consciousness—I'd say that's art.

I had read Matilde Amaya's cookbook, *La Cocina Gitana*, back in New York. I've met her son, Antonio Carmona, one of the most talented flamenco musicians alive. I've thought about her food. And I sent Claudia, Mark, and Gwyneth to find her in Andalucía—I had them search Granada, had them drive to Malaga. No luck. Finally, I found her in Madrid—thank God, because she's fantastic.

Considered the matriarch of *la cocina gitana* (gypsy cooking), Matilde is a woman of incredible wisdom and spirit, and she has the most dangerously beautiful eyes in the Iberian Peninsula. She married when she was twenty and, in her words, "didn't even know how to fry an egg." Her husband wanted her to cook his favorite dishes, so he set her up with his favorite cook: his mother. Matilde watched her mother-in-law carefully and, in turn, became an expert cook, a confident and skilled *mujer de la cocina* (woman of the kitchen).

She walks into the kitchen in an orange polka-dotted apron—as if she hadn't captured my heart already—and begins to describe gypsy cooking. It's worth knowing that gypsies live everywhere, but their cooking, not to mention their music, ties them together. *La comida gitana* can be found all over, but it has a certain consistency and personality that makes it unmistakable. There's a commonality to the food. It's not afraid of salt or spice, and it relies on inexpensive ingredients: onions, garlic, peppers, salt cod. It's common food, but courageous food, unabashedly flavorful and generously satisfying. A dish of *comida gitana* will both excite and nourish you. Watching Matilde, I soon realize that my style of cooking is pretty similar—I start nearly everything with olive oil, garlic, and onions. Perhaps I, too, am a gypsy cook.

RECIPE

GYPSY POTAGE

This traditional Christmastime soup, made with salt cod, chickpeas, and spinach, displays the gypsy kitchen's particular combination of modesty and brazen flavor. Not unlike flamenco, the great music whose roots lie deep in gypsy culture, la comida gitana is soulful and rhythmic, heartwarming, and satisfying to be around. Look for skin-on bacalao—the skin will add flavor and texture to the thick, hearty soup.

SERVES 6

Two 14-ounce can chickpeas, drained and rinsed

¼ cup extra-virgin olive oil

2 garlic cloves, peeled

½ large Spanish onion, cut into small dice

Scant 1 cup tomato puree

2 tablespoons sweet *pimentón* (Spanish smoked paprika)

Pinch of saffron threads

1 pound baby spinach

2 tablespoons finely chopped Italian parsley

½ teaspoon cumin seeds

1½ pounds skin-on, boneless bacalao (salt cod), soaked in water for 3 days (change the water twice a day)

5 cups water

Put the chickpeas into a large heavy pot, add 2 cups cold water, and bring to a simmer.

Meanwhile, heat the olive oil in a large sauté pan over medium heat. Add the garlic cloves and cook until they are just beginning to color. Add 1 garlic clove to the chickpeas, and reserve the other. Add the onions to the skillet and cook until softened and beginning to brown, about 10 minutes. Add the tomato puree and pimentón and cook for about 5 minutes, until the tomato puree is slightly reduced.

Add the onion mixture to the chickpeas (add a bit of the chickpea liquid to the skillet to help get all the onion and tomato mixture—don't waste a bit!), then add the saffron. Add the spinach, stirring until it wilts.

Using a mortar and pestle, mash the reserved garlic clove, the parsley, and cumin to a paste. Add the paste to the soup, along with the drained bacalao, breaking it into large pieces. Add the remaining 3 cups water, bring to a rolling boil, and cook for 10 minutes. Taste for salt and add it if necessary, then turn off the heat, cover, and let stand for about 10 minutes before serving.

GYPSY SALAD

This salad, like the soup, is made with bacalao, salt cod. Combined with eggs, potatoes, and oranges, it's every shade of white and yellow. After one taste, I ask Matilde if she has a boyfriend. She responds with laughter and tells me she's already a great-grandmother. I figured it couldn't hurt to ask.

SERVES 4 TO 6

3 medium waxy potatoes, boiled, peeled, and cut into ¼-inch-thick slices

½ large Spanish onion, thinly sliced

2 hard-boiled eggs, peeled and sliced

A handful of black olives (whatever you like)

1 orange, peeled and cut into ¼-inch-thick slices

½ pound skinless, boneless bacalao (salt cod), soaked in water for 3 days (change the water twice a day), drained, and broken into bite-sized pieces

¼ cup extra-virgin olive oil

Sea salt (optional)

Combine all the ingredients (except the optional salt) in a bowl and toss gently to mix. Season with salt if necessary. That's it.

DUQUESA DE ALBA'S PALACE

Don't ask how, but, incredibly, we get access to the Duquesa de Alba's palace. Right off a main drag in Madrid, we drive up to what appears to be a movie set. It's almost a caricature of a palace, complete with parrots squawking inside and fancy cars in the driveway. The rooms are carpeted with embroidered rugs and filled with antique chairs, and the walls are covered with paintings by Titian, Goya, and Fra Angelico. We walk past a desk that belonged to Napoleon III and see that it's covered with small perfume vials and other tzotchkes. I wonder who dusts all of this.

It's said that the Duquesa has more royal blood than even the Spanish king. If they bump into each other, he has to bow to her. She also has so many possessions that it's said if she lined up everything she owned, the collection would circle all of Spain. We leave soon after arriving, afraid to break anything but honored to have stepped inside.

FAVORITE TAPAS

GWYNETH:

PAN CON TOMATE Y ANCHOAS
(bread with tomato and anchovies).

ACEITUNAS
(olives).

MANCHEGO.

MARIO:

PERCEBES
(gooseneck barnacles).

PINCHO MORUÑO
(a small skewer loaded with paprika-marinated meat).

CLAUDIA:

Impossible to choose!

OLIVES.

HAM CROQUETAS.

PATATAS BRAVAS
(fried potatoes with spicy tomato sauce and aioli).

PIMIENTOS DEL PADRÓN
(small green peppers grilled and sprinkled with salt).

TORTILLA ESPAÑOLA.

GAMBAS AL AJILLO
(shrimp with garlic and olive oil).

MARK:

I like it all, especially
ANCHOAS.

WHAT WE'RE LOOKING FORWARD TO

Our trip is winding down and we decide to stay in
Madrid, to end full circle.

13

MADRID AL FINALE

WHERE WE'RE GOING

Way back in Galicia, Gwyneth came up with the idea that we should have a cooking competition, with her and me against Mark and Claudia. We haven't been putting it off, we've been preparing. Madrid is the perfect backdrop for our ultimate show-down. The competition is followed by exploring a lot more of Madrid—good food, drinks, architecture, and more food.

WHAT WE'RE EATING

MARIO'S AJO BLANCO p. 339, CLAUDIA'S SPAGHETTI p. 340, MARK'S ALMOND-CRUSTED FISH p. 343, GARLIC CHIPS p. 343, GWYNETH'S TAKE ON A "GOOD HUMOR" BAR p. 344, GWYNETH'S ALMOND HORCHATA p. 346, Roast Chicken, COCIDO p. 353

We go to my friend Sergi Arola's restaurant in Madrid, Gastro, to have the ultimate battle—what we will call "Titanium Chef." Gwyneth and I team up with Sergi's chef friend Sacha, and Sergi joins Claudia and Mark. The secret ingredient: Spanish almonds! The battle's on.

Sergi is supercool, maybe even too cool. He enters the kitchen in dress pants and a Foo Fighters T-shirt, aviator glasses, and a slick brown leather jacket. Sacha looks more as if he just came down from a mountain somewhere; he wears an old suede hat to "hide the shine and to keep the ideas from falling out of [my] head." Gwyneth is excited and calls out, "¡A cocinar! ¡Venga, vamos! (Let's cook! Let's go, let's go!)" The kitchen is energized and the competition totally friendly. Mark asks what the rules are, and I tell him not to burn anything, including himself.

MARK: Do I start the distracting now or wait until later?

MARIO: Don't you have something to cook, Bitty?

GWYNETH: He can't cook, don't you know that?

MARIO: As long as we don't burn anything, we'll be fine—they're going to burn everything.

MARK: We're not burning anything!

SERGI: Cut it very thin, all the same size.

MARK: That's not going to happen. I'm a journalist.

A glass breaks . . .

GWYNETH: Mazel tov!

MARIO: Was it Claudia?

MARK: No, it was Sergi.

CLAUDIA: Thanks for the vote of confidence, Batali.

MARK: Oh no. We have to start again.

MARIO: Why? Did the plastic wrap break on your take-out container?

MARIO: This is a melon baller? This is surgical equipment!

MARK: Your whole thing is going to fail because you don't have the right melon baller?

MARIO: The mini balls will work. Not my size, but that's the kind of guy I am.

GWYNETH: So you're saying you will have mini balls?

MARIO: In Spain, size doesn't matter.

MARK: So, this is the second time you've ever been in a kitchen. How's it going?

CLAUDIA: You know what, I'm doing great!

MARK: You look so relaxed. You're not upset, not uptight. You're a natural.

MARIO: Obviously they have cooking schools in Cleveland.

MARIO: Six minutes left! Enough to burn the garlic!

MARK: Yeah, I already did that.

Mario's
AJO BLANCO

Ajo blanco is a very traditional version of gazpacho, but it isn't as well known as its tomato-based sibling. It's simple and extremely satisfying; a perfectly refreshing cold soup that celebrates almonds.

SERVES 4

1 cup blanched whole almonds

2 garlic cloves, minced

½ cup sherry vinegar

4 ice cubes

1 cup extra-virgin olive oil

Sea salt

20 seedless green grapes, halved

Grated zest of 2 lemons

Put the almonds in a small saucepan, cover with cold water, and bring to a boil. Turn off the heat and let stand for 10 minutes, to soften slightly.

Drain the almonds, transfer to a blender or food processor, and add the garlic, vinegar, and 4 cups cold water. Blend until smooth, about 1 minute. With the motor running, add the ice cubes, then add the olive oil in a slow, steady stream, blending until thoroughly combined. Season with salt, and refrigerate until chilled.

Divide the grapes and zest between four small bowls, pour the soup over, and serve.

¿QUÉ es?

ALMENDRA: *Almendra* is the Spanish word for "almond." Most of Spain's almonds go into *turrón*, a sweet, nougaty candy that's consumed in huge quantities around Christmas. But almonds seem to always be around in Spain. They pop up, sprinkled with salt, at bars with your cocktails; they arrive in small bags on every Spanish flight; they are ground into all sorts of cakes and pastries; and they accompany most cheeses and fruits.

CLAUDIA'S SPAGHETTI
with vegetables, truffles, and almonds

This wasn't the most almond-centric dish, but you can't go wrong with fava beans, morels, and a healthy shaving of truffle.

SERVES 4 AS AN APPETIZER

½ pound spaghetti

¼ cup extra-virgin olive oil

½ cup morels

½ cup peeled fava beans

½ cup fresh peas

½ cup toasted almonds,
   finely chopped

1 small black truffle

Bring a large pot of generously salted water to a boil. Drop in the spaghetti and cook until perfectly al dente.

Meanwhile, heat the olive oil in a medium sauté pan over medium heat. Add the morels and cook for about 4 minutes, or until beginning to soften. Add the fava beans and peas and sauté for a minute or two, until just tender.

Drain the pasta, reserving a cup of its cooking water, and add to the vegetables. Stir to combine, adding some of the reserved pasta water as needed. Divide among four bowls, sprinkle with the almonds, and shave or grate the truffle over. Serve immediately.

Mark's
ALMOND-CRUSTED FISH

Bittman pulled through—his fish was totally simple but really tasty. The almonds lent a great crunch and the herbs filled your mouth with incredible flavor.

SERVES 2

1 cup finely chopped blanched
    almonds

1 teaspoon finely chopped thyme

1 teaspoon finely chopped
    rosemary

1 tablespoon finely chopped
    lemon zest

1 cup all-purpose flour

2 eggs

2 tablespoons unsalted butter

2 tablespoons extra-virgin
    olive oil

Two 6-ounce firm white fish fillets
    (whatever's fresh and good)

Kosher salt and freshly ground
    black pepper

Garlic Chips (recipe follows)

Lemon wedges for serving

Mix together the almonds, thyme, rosemary, and lemon zest. Put the flour in a shallow bowl; lightly beat the eggs in another shallow bowl.

Heat the butter and oil in a large skillet over medium-high heat until foaming. Season the fish with salt and pepper. Dredge in the flour, then dip into the eggs, letting the excess drip off, and dredge in the almond mixture, turning to coat. Add to the pan and cook, turning once, for 3 to 4 minutes per side, or until the fish is opaque throughout and the almonds are nicely toasted. Sprinkle with the garlic chips and serve with lemon wedges.

garlic chips

Bittman made a garnish!

¼ cup extra-virgin olive oil

3 garlic cloves, thinly sliced

Combine the oil and garlic in a small saucepan and cook over low heat until the garlic slices are golden brown and crispy. Remove the garlic with a slotted spoon and drain on paper towels. Save the oil for a salad dressing or aïoli, or for drizzling over vegetables, plain grilled fish, or whatever you like.

Gwyneth's take on a
"GOOD HUMOR" BAR

Gwyneth loves "Good Humor" Toasted Almond Bars, and she created this assembled dessert in homage. The sugar-coated almonds are delicious on just about anything, from yogurt to a salad, or alongside cheese, or even eaten out of hand.

SERVES 4

¼ cup unblanched
    whole almonds

¼ cup sugar

1 tablespoon extra-virgin
    olive oil

1 pint high-quality almond
    ice cream

4 teaspoons amaretto

Toss the almonds with the sugar and oil in a medium skillet and cook over medium heat, stirring occasionally, until the sugar melts and the almonds are toasted. Transfer to a plate and let cool, then chop the almonds.

Divide the ice cream among four bowls, sprinkle with the chopped almonds, and drizzle a teaspoon of amaretto over each.

Gwyneth's
ALMOND HORCHATA

Based on the classic Spanish horchata *made with tiger nuts, this almond version has a sweet, clean taste that isn't at all heavy or rich.*

SERVES 2

1 cup blanched whole almonds, soaked overnight in 2 cups cold water

1 vanilla bean, split

¼ cup sugar

¾ teaspoon ground cinnamon

 Cayenne pepper

2 cinnamon sticks

Put the almonds and their soaking water in a saucepan and bring to a boil. Transfer to a blender and blend until smooth. Strain through a very fine strainer (discard the solids), and pour the almond milk back into the clean blender. Scrape the seeds from the vanilla bean and add them to the blender, along with the sugar and ground cinnamon; blend well. Pour into two glasses, sprinkle with cayenne, and garnish with the cinnamon sticks.

Sure, Madrid is a bit of a regal city, but there's a lot of new architecture and renovation happening, and it seems that Madrid is beginning to take on a lot of new without losing any of the old. One of the best examples is the Matadero, a huge complex of buildings in the southern part of the city built in 1910. The word *matadero* translates as "slaughterhouse," its function until the 1990s, but now the Matadero is being reinvented as an arts center, complete with a design school and exhibition spaces. The neighborhood is still sort of low-end, but it's becoming hip. Kind of like New York City's SoHo in the late 1980s or Williamsburg in the past decade.

When you walk into the Matadero, it's wonderful to see that the team behind the renovations has maintained the industrial character of the original structure. We take a quick look at an exhibition of package design, and it becomes evident that even in food containers, Spaniards push design to the edge, even over the edge. Spain is ahead.

Another example of reinvention is the Caixa Forum, a new arts space located on the site of an old gas station. The outside is as impressive as its interior: one wall is dedicated to the world's largest vertical garden, designed by Patrick Blanc, a French botanist. The wall has more than 120 different types of plants, and a very complicated watering system is involved. It reminds us a bit of Jeff Koons's flower-coated dog outside of the Guggenheim in Bilbao.

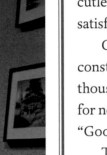
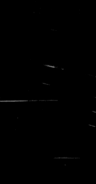

· RESTAURANT ·

CASA MINGO

· MADRID ·

Claudia has heard about a great chicken place called Casa Mingo, so she, Mark, and I head over. It's fantastic. Signs on the walls explicitly prohibit singing, and the waiters wear short-sleeved white shirts and small black bow ties. The room is built of dark brown wood and the ceiling is high. The tables are simple, and once we sit down, everyone is brought crusty bread, water, and cutlery. Being near a university, Casa Mingo draws students because it's fast, satisfying, and cheap. In other words, the perfect road-trip joint.

Casa Mingo opened in 1887 as a sort of cafeteria for the workers who were constructing the North Train Station down the street. To this day, they sell thousands of chickens a week. When we ask the waiter, who has worked here for nearly thirty years, what keeps business going, he replies with confidence, "Good ingredients." I couldn't agree more.

The menu is short and offers, beside the chicken, mostly Asturian-style food, including our new favorite bean stew, *fabada*. In accordance, we order a bottle of Asturian cider. While we wait for our food, Claudia and I attempt to give Mark a mini Spanish lesson, but he's quite hopeless. For example, he thinks the word for "fork" is *forketa*. Luckily the food arrives quickly. We have roast chicken, homemade chorizo cooked in cider, *callos* (stewed tripe), a big wedge of Cabrales blue cheese, and a really addictive dish called *asadillo y ventresca*. Funny that when the gastronomic inner lane is being driven by Claudia, the place known for chicken ends up having great tripe and tuna. She has never tried tripe and Mark, in his ongoing pursuit to get her to try all outrageous foods, encourages her. She agrees for the sake of experience but is noticeably hesitant. After one bite, she pushes it aside: "Not loving *callos* isn't a crime." We continue to eat, and the chicken's salty, crispy skin makes all the sense in the world with the sweet cider. Our stomachs padded, we're ready to enjoy Madrid's nightlife.

¿QUÉ es?

ASADILLO Y VENTRESCA: We had a delicious small plate at Casa Mingo called *asadillo y ventresca*. It consists of a rich *pisto* (pureed roasted vegetables) with oily canned Spanish tuna and wedges of hard-boiled eggs. It's a simple and satisfying dish. I think it'd be great sandwiched inside a crusty roll.

**MARIO:
You have
to live
life to
its full
chorizo.**

Mark, Claudia, and I had a crazy evening. The next morning, while Claudia sleeps it off, Mark and I head to Restaurante La Bola, which was established in 1870 and is one of the best old-fashioned, traditional joints around. The walls are wood paneled and lined with photos; it's intimate, it's warm, it's totally comfortable. We've come to eat *cocido*, the famous chickpea stew that's known as a Madrileño hangover cure. You make it by simmering chickpeas with chicken, beef, veal, pork, chorizo, and spices over a coal fire for hours. It's staggeringly delicious. You can eat it all together or as two courses— the broth and then the meat and beans. We opt for the second choice and enjoy the broth first with noodles. It's smoky and red from the chorizo, and we add raw onion and pickled peppers to our bowls. Then we dig into the chickpeas and meat, with a few boiled potatoes and cabbage on the side. Mark gets a bit sappy and starts saying things like, "You can taste the smoke, you can taste the history."

COCIDO
(madrileño hangover cure)

*This combination of chickpeas and just about the entire butcher's case is
Madrid's traditional hangover remedy.*

SERVES 10 TO 12

1 pound beef brisket,
    cut into 2-inch chunks

½ pound slab bacon,
    cut into 4 pieces

1 pound beef marrow bones
    (cut into 1- to 2-inch pieces
    by the butcher)

½ pound Spanish chorizo,
    cut into 1-inch pieces

One 2- to 3-pound boiling
    chicken, cut into 8 pieces

1 small onion, peeled and
    studded with 3 cloves

1 head garlic, cut in half across
    the bulb

2 bay leaves

2 teaspoons crushed
    black peppercorns

1 pound dried chickpeas,
    soaked overnight in water
    to cover and drained

1 Savoy cabbage,
    cut into 8 wedges

1 pound small boiling potatoes

Cooked noodles, chopped
    raw onion, and pickled
    peppers for serving

Put the meats, chicken, onion, garlic, bay leaves, and peppercorns in a large stockpot, cover with water, and bring to a boil. Skim off the foam, add the chickpeas, lower the heat, cover, and simmer gently for 2 hours, or until the chickpeas are soft.

Meanwhile, bring a large pot of salted water to a boil. Add the cabbage and potatoes and cook until tender, about 25 minutes; drain and keep warm.

Ladle the broth from the meats into bowls (keep the meats warm in a little broth) and serve as a first course with the noodles, chopped onion, and peppers. Serve the meats and chickpeas as a second course with the potatoes and cabbage, moistening everything with a bit of broth.

EL ESCORIAL

We wander around Escorial, the Royal Monastery of San Lorenzo el Real, and it's much prettier than I remembered from my tenth-grade field trip. This time, with a far better guide, the chapel seems so much more of the focus, and it looks very beautiful from this perspective. When we came as a high-school class, Escorial was enrobed in fog. This time we can see it both as we approach it and when we drive away, which gives it a magical royal-palace feel. Later we have a mediocre lunch of greasy lamb chops and cardboard octopus—but straight ahead is the *fútbol* game, where great sandwiches are promised.

¿QUÉ es?

ALCALÁ: We spent one morning in Alcalá de Henares, known simply as Alcalá. A small medieval town, Alcalá has been preserved as a UNESCO World Heritage Site. It's worth noting that this is where Cervantes was born. It's also next door to one of Spain's largest landfills—try not to go on a windy day.

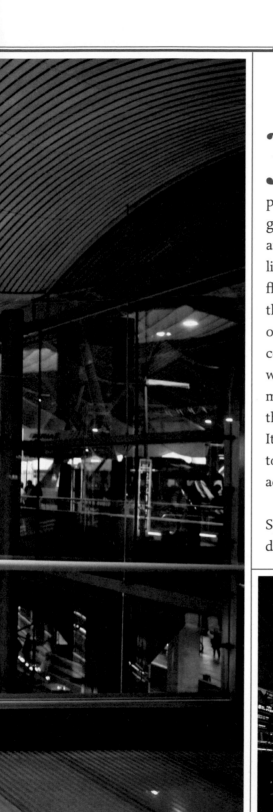

It was wonderful to meet and talk with Carlos Lamela and Simon Smithson, two of the main architects involved in the design of the airport. It's a fascinating project, and they first approached it from four perspectives: getting into the airport, checking in, going through security, and boarding the plane. They evaluated each issue in terms of limiting chaos and creating calm. They also approached the flip side: getting off the plane, retrieving luggage, and leaving the airport. For each of these three parts, they concentrated on bringing natural light to the customer. Their overall use of color and light is well conceived. The most surprising thing was how much bamboo they used—the whole subceiling is made of bamboo slats. Above, there is an acoustic treatment that makes all the hard surfaces and noise situation moot. It was quiet. The philosophy behind the construction was to create calm, and the architects said most of this goal was achieved through lighting and noise control.

Touring the airport showed just another example of Spain's thoughtful and forward-thinking approach to art, design, and construction.

WHAT'S THE FASTEST YOU DROVE ON THE TRIP?

GWYNETH:

I love driving,
I'M A VERY FAST DRIVER.

MARIO:
245 KM/HR
(but I'm not as fast as Gwyneth).

CLAUDIA:
120 KM/HR
and I am not ashamed.

MARK:
220 KM/HR.

RESOURCES:
Páginas Amarillas
(Yellow Pages)

Paradores, *located all over Spain, are a national chain of hotels and other hostelries, located often in old palaces, castles, convents, and monasteries, are part of a national chain that was initiated by Alfonso XIII in order to promote tourism.*

ÁVILA HOTELS
Parador de Ávila
Marqués de Canales de Chozas, 2
920-211-340
www.parador.es
A sixteenth-century palace, this parador sits conveniently in the center of Ávila and has a beautiful garden.

Hotel Ávila Golf
Carretera Cebreros, km 3
920-359-200
www.fontecruz.com/avila-golf-hotel
Any hotel with the word "golf" in it is a plus if your name is Mario Batali.

ÁVILA RESTAURANTS
El Almacén
Carretera de Salamanca, 6
920-211-026
This restaurant in an old warehouse boasts a humongous wine list.

El Molino de la Losa
Calle Bajada de la Losa, 12
920-21-11-01
www.elmolinodelalosa.com
A converted mill, El Molino has great Ribera del Duero wines and interesting local cheeses.

BARCELONA HOTELS
AC Miramar
Plaza Carlos Ibáñez, 3
93-281-16-00
www.ac-hotels.com
A beautiful hotel at the end of Parc de Montjuïc. Very modern and sleek.

Hotel Claris
Carrer Pau Claris, 150
93-487-62-62
www.derbyhotels.es
Just off Paseo de Gracia and steps away from Plaza Catalunya, this has a rooftop pool and a hipster vibe.

Gran Derby Hotel
Carrer Loreto, 28
93-445-25-44
www.derbyhotels.es
Located between Avenida Diagonal and the Sarrià district, this hotel has a rooftop pool and a cool mix of old-and-new design in its forty-one rooms.

BARCELONA RESTAURANTS
Inopia
Calle Tamarit, 104
93-424-52-31
www.barinopia.com
The best tapas we've had!

La Clara
Gran Vía Corts Catalanes, 442
93-289-34-60
www.laclararestaurant.com
When you need some fried brains . . . .

Bar Pinxto
Mercat de la Boquería
93-318-20-17
www.boqueria.info
Breakfast and lunch only. No reservations, no tables, just a bar, where you must order the chipirones (baby squid), the cap y pota (a Catalan dish of veal's head and hooves slowly braised in a clay pot), and dream the Batali dream, with thumbs-up.

Kresala (formerly Jean Luc Figueras)
Calle Santa Teresa, 10
93-41-52-877
www.kresalarestaurant.com
One of my favorite of the upscale, new-idea places. The food still has much of the traditional flavors of Catalan cooking, but the presentations are modern.

Can Pineda
Calle Sant Joan de Malta, 55
93-308-30-81
Insider info sent us to this excellent locals-only place. It's almost impossible to get in, but it's worth the effort.

BILBAO HOTELS
Gran Hotel Domine
Alameda Mazarredo, 61
944-253-300
www.hoteles-silken.com/ghdb
It's directly across the street from the Guggenheim—talk about a good view! It's extremely hip and there's an amusing fountain in the lobby made of tableware.

Miró Hotel
Alameda Mazarredo, 77
94-661-18-80
www.mirohotelbilbao.com
Designed by Antoni Miró, this is down the street from the Guggenheim and is chic, comfortable, and modern.

BILBAO RESTAURANTS
Zuga
94-415-0321
Plaza Nueva, 4
Innovative tapas, with a line of strollers parked outside.

Casa Víctor Montes
Plaza Nueva, 8
94-415-5603
Old-school montaditos (see page 112).

Bukoi
Calle de la Esperanza, 18
94-479-0093
When you're in the mood for jamón.

CAMBADOS RESTAURANT
Casa Pintos
Travesia Montiño, 14
986-542-435
For perfect fresh seafood—it's down the street from the sea.

CÓRDOBA HOTEL
Parador La Arruzafa
Avenida de la Arruzafa
957-275-900
www.parador.es
This parador is on the ruins of a summer palace.

CÓRDOBA RESTAURANT
Sociedad de Plateros
Calle María Auxiliadora, 25
957-470-304
www.sociedadplateros.com
Good food, nice atmosphere—it's the neighborhood restaurant you wish you had in your own neighborhood.

GRANADA HOTEL
Parador de San Francisco
Calle Real de la Alhambra
95-822-14-40
www.parador.es
This parador is located in a fifteenth-century convent . . . in the Alhambra!

GRANADA RESTAURANTS
Restaurant Rincón de la Aurora
95-232-49-16
Plaza San Miguel Bajo, 7
Wonderful food that reminds you how close Granada is to Morocco.

Restaurant Morayma
Calle Pianista García Carrillo, 2
95-822-82-90
Amazing views of the Alhambra, and some good fideos too.

La Última Ola
Paseo Puerta del Mar, 17
18690 Almuñecar
95-863-00-18
Spectacular seafood on the Costa del Sol.

LA RIOJA HOTELS
Hotel Marqués de Riscal
Calle Torrea, 1
01340 Elciego
94-518-08-80
www.starwoodhotels.com
Designed by Frank Gehry and one of my favorite hotels in the world.

Parador de Calahorra
Paseo Mercadal
26500 Calahorra
94-113-03-58
www.parador.es
Situated in an old red brick cathedral in the middle of a beautiful garden.

Parador de Santo Domingo de la Calzada
Plaza del Santo, 3
26250 Santo Domingo de la Calzada
94-134-03-00
www.parador.es
Once a hospital, dating back to the twelfth century, this regal building is brightly colored (and near a golf course).

LUGO HOTELS
A Parada das Bestas
(Casa Rural)
Pidre, 27
27207 Palas de Rei
689-119-521
www.aparadadasbestas.com
Tell María and Suso that we sent you!

Parador de Monforte de Lemos
Plaza Luis Góngora y Argote
27400 Monforte de Lemos
98-241-84-84
www.parador.es
A seventeenth-century Benedictine monastery set at the highest point in Monforte de Lemos.

Parador de Ribadeo
Calle Amador Fernández, 7
98-212-885
27700 Ribadeo
www.parador.es
Sleep on an estuary! This parador is a large, traditional Galician house located at the mouth of the Ribadeo.

Parador Condes de Vilalba
Calle Valeriano Valdesuso
27800 Vilalba
98-251-00-11
www.parador.es
Just your ordinary fifteenth-century medieval fortress. Stay in one of the tower's six rooms, not the new building.

MADRID HOTELS
AC Santa Mauro
Calle Zurbano, 36
913-196-900
www.ac-hotels.com
It's chic, it's luxe, it's very, very cool.

Hotel de las Letras
Gran Vía, 11
915-237-980
www.hoteldelasletras.com
Situated in a nineteenth-century townhouse near the Puerta del Sol, Hotel de las Letras is as charming as it is comfortable.

Hotel Puerta América
Avenida de América, 41
917-445-400
www.hoteles-silken.com
A truly innovative and intriguing hotel. Each floor was designed by a different world-famous architect; everyone from Norman Foster to Zaha Hadid has a level to call his or her own.

Parador de Chinchón
Calle de Los Huertos, 1
28370 Chinchón
918-408-36
www.parador.es
This former Augustan convent in the old Chinchón neighborhood, 32 miles southeast of Madrid, offers peace and quiet, as well as a wonderful sopa de ajo (garlic soup) in its restaurant.

MADRID RESTAURANTS
Casa Lucio
Cava Baja, 35
913-653-252
www.casalucio.es
It's the champion.

Reche
Calle de Don Ramón de la Cruz, 49
915-779-379
Cool, modern Spanish cooking in a hip setting.

Antigua Casa Ángel Sierra
Calle de Gravina, 11
91-531-0126
Well known for its boquerones (anchovies), Casa Ángel Sierra is an old-fashioned taberna (tavern).

La Terraza, Casino de Madrid
Calle Alcalá, 15
915-321-275
www.casinodemadrid.es
For exceptional "molecular gastronomy."

Sergi Arola Gastro
Calle Zubano, 31
913-102-169
www.sergiarola.es
This place is totally exciting, even when there's not a cooking competition going on in the kitchen.

Casa Mingo
Paseo de la Florida, 34
915-477-918
Whether you're a student or an executive, the great, cheap chicken can't be beat. Wash it down with sweet cider and have a plate of callos (stewed tripe) and asadillo y ventresca (pisto with tuna and eggs) while you're there.

Taberna La Bola
Calle Bola, 5
915-417-164
www.labola.es
The best cocido (chickpea stew) in town.

Casa Fidel
Calle de Escorial, 6
915-317-736
A small, quiet restaurant with deliciously simple food. The callos (tripe) with peppercorns is especially good.

MALLORCA HOTELS
La Residencia
Finca Son Canals
07179 Deià
www.hotellaresidencia.com
800-237-1236
Beyond beautiful. It's where I always stay.

Hotel Ca's Sant
Finca Ca's Sant Cami ses Fontanelles, 34
07100 Sóller
971-63-02-98
www.cas-sant.com
A country hotel near the port area of Sóller, where the best shrimp are caught.

MALLORCA RESTAURANTS
El Olivo at La Residencia
Finca Son Canals
07179 Deià
800-237-1236
www.hotellaresidencia.com
Smart food and wonderful service.

Can Joan de S'aigo
Calle Baró Santa María del Sepulcre, 5
07007 Palma de Mallorca
971-710-759
You must try the ice creams and, of course, the ensaimadas. A great place for breakfast before a round or two of golf.

Restaurant Malvasiá
Calle Joan Bauzá, 43
07007 Palma de Mallorca
971-240-086
Go for the food, the wine, and the warmth. Try the habas (fava beans) and the hake baked in coca (a pizza-like bread).

MENORCA HOTELS
Hotel Port Mahón
Avenida Port de Maó
07701 Mahón
902-110-111
A reliable, good hotel; most important, it's near where they make great Mahón (Maó) cheese.

Hotel La Quinta
Gran Via Son Xoriguer
07769 Ciutadella
971-055-000
A five-star hotel with beautiful colonial architecture.

MENORCA RESTAURANT
Restaurante Can'Aguedet
Calle Lapanto, 22–30
971-37-53-91
The older lady with the blue rinse in her hair is not to be underestimated—she's the matriarch of the restaurant and will take good care of you.

OVIEDO HOTELS
AC Forum
Plaza Ferroviarios, 1
985-965-488
www.ac-hotels.com
Conveniently located and reliable.

Hotel Occidental de la Reconquista
Gil de Jaz, 16
985-241-100
www.hoteldelareconquista.com
Five stars, totally central, and luxurious.

Parador de Cangas de Onís
Monasterio de San Pedro de Villanueva
33550 Cangas de Onís
985-849-402
www.parador.es
Originally a monastery constructed in 746 (the rooms have been updated!), and the setting can't be beat.

OVIEDO RESTAURANTS
Casa Fermín
Calle San Francisco, 8
985-216-497
An elegant old-school restaurant.

La Sidrería
Plaza Pedro Miñor, 4
985-244-905
Drink up!

RIBERA DEL DUERO HOTEL
Hotel Ribera del Duero
Avenida Escalona, 17
47300 Penafiel
983-873-111
www.hotelriberadelduero.com
This hotel was once a flour mill. It's been beautifully restored, with many wonderful old details preserved. Try to get a room with exposed beams.

ROSES RESTAURANTS
Rafa's
Calle Sant Sebastià, 56
972-25-40-03
The best fish!

El Bulli
Cala Montjoi
972-15-04-57
www.elbulli.com/
Ferran Adrià's pilgrimage site—and worth it. It's open only from April until September and reservations are accepted only on one day in October.

SALAMANCA HOTELS
Parador de Salamanca
Calle Teso de la Feria, 2
923-192-082
www.parador.es
Let's cut to the chase—this parador has a golf course.

Parador de Ciudad Rodrigo
Plaza Catillo, 1
37500 Ciudad Rodrigo
923-460-150
www.parador.es
A fourteenth-century castle overlooking the Águeda River, about fifty miles from Salamanca, this parador is a thinker's paradise—sit in the courtyard or on the grounds and contemplate the landscape.

SALAMANCA RESTAURANTS
Trento
San Pablo, 58
923-261-818
Set inside the Palacio de Castellanos, this stylish restaurant has good food and a pleasant ambience.

La Hoja
Pasaje Coliseum, 19
923-264-882
A favorite local chef, Alberto López Oliva, serves traditional food with a twist.

SAN SEBASTIÁN HOTELS
Parador de Hondarribia
Plaza de Armas del Castillo
20280 Hondarribia
943-645-50
www.parador.es
Don't be put off by the forbidding exterior—this old medieval fortress houses one of the most comfortable paradors around.

Hotel María Cristina
Oquendo, 1
943-437-600
A beautiful, luxurious hotel in an old Belle Epoque building.

SAN SEBASTIÁN RESTAURANTS
Arzak
Avenida Alcalde Elosegui, 273
943-278-465
www.arzak.info
More than a must-go—it's an absolutely no-doubt-about-it, totally, completely must-go.

La Cepa
Calle de Agosto/Abuztuaren, 31
943-431-973
Perfect pintxos.

Ganbara
Calle San Jerónimo, 21
943-422-575
Perfect mushrooms.

SANTIAGO HOTELS
Santiago de Compostela
Plaza do Obradoiro, 1
981-582-200
www.parador.es
Considered to be the oldest hotel in the world, this is located in the same plaza as the cathedral. Not coincidentally, it was a hospital and refuge for pilgrims during the fifteenth century.

AC Palacio del Carmen
Calle Oblatas
981-552-444
www.ac-hotels.com
A former convent, this is a comfortable contemporary hotel near the center of the city.

SANTIAGO RESTAURANTS
Restaurante 42
Calle de Franco, 42
981–57–06–65
Wonderful seafood and tapas—percebes, killer berberechos, pickled green peppers, patatas bravas, and jamón—and lots of orujo.

Sexto II
Calle do Franco, 23
981-56-05-24
We ate berberechos, steamed sweet red shrimp, grilled lenguado (sole), and ensalada mixta drowned in vinegar and olive oil—and we couldn't have been happier.

SANT POL DE MAR RESTAURANT
Carme Ruscalleda Sant Pau
Calle Nou, 10
93-760-0662
www.ruscalleda.com
Three stars on the Costa Brava. Must, must go!

SEGOVIA HOTELS
Parador de Segovia
Carretera de Valladolid
921-443-737
www.parador.es
Comfortable, basic rooms, with a great view of the city.

Parador de la Granja
Calle de los Infantes, 3
40100 La Granja de San Ildefonso
921-010-750
www.parador.es
An old royal property about seven miles from Segovia, this parador consists of the prince's house (now the hotel) and bodyguard barracks (now a conference center).

SEGOVIA RESTAURANTS
Mesón de Cándido
Plaza del Azoguejo, 5
921-425-911
www.mesondecandido.es
The place to go for cochinillo (suckling pig).

Restaurante Duque
Calle Cervantes, 12
921-462-487
www.restauranteduque.es
It's been around since 1895, and the food is hip—okay, hip for 1895. Slow-roasted meats, boiled beans, and mounds of potatoes.

TEMBLEQUE HOTELS
Hotel Queso
Carretera Andalucía, km 102
925-145-063
It's always wise to stay anywhere named Hotel Cheese.

Hotel La Purísima
Calle de la Ermita Purísima
925-145-036
It's a hostel, but it's comfortable and, of course, completely affordable.

TEMBLEQUE RESTAURANT
Mesón Venta de Tiembles
Plaza Mayor, 11
925-145-234
It's one of two restaurants in town. Luckily it's good.

TOLEDO HOTELS
Parador de Toledo
Cerro del Emperador
925-221-850
www.parador.es
This is one of the most well-known paradors, and it deserves the praise. Built on the edge of a hill, it's located where El Greco supposedly sat to catch the greatest view of the city. The restaurant serves some of Toledo's most well known foods, including partridge and marzipan.

Palacio Eugenia de Montijo
Plaza del Juego de Pelota, 7
www.fontecruz.com/eugenia-de-montijo
925-274-690
Perhaps the most luxurious hotel in Toledo.

Hotel El Pintor El Greco
Alamillos del Tránsito, 13
925-285-191
www.hotel-pintorelgreco.com
The charm of this hotel, located in the Jewish
Quarter in what was once a bakery, is the result
of thoughtful and careful restoration.

TOLEDO RESTAURANTS
Asador Adolfo
Calle de la Granada, 6
925-252-472
www.grupoadolfo.com
When in Toledo, you must try Adolfo's food. This is
his most celebrated restaurant.

La Perdiz
Calle Reyes Católicos, 7
925-252-919
www.grupoadolfo.com
Run by Adolfo's family, this restaurant in the old
Jewish Quarter is named for the Toledan partridge.

Taberna el Antojo
Plaza de San Juan de los Reyes, 11
925-210-699
This is Adolfo's favorite tapas bar.

VALENCIA HOTELS
Palau de la Mar
Navarro Reverter, 14
963-162-884
www.avantgardehotels.com
A renovated palace; the rooms have the glitz of old
architecture and the sleekness of modern design.

Parador El Saler
Avenida de los Pinares, 151
46012 El Saler
961-611-186
www.parador.es
A brand-new parador situated on a golf course next
to the sea.

VALENCIA RESTAURANTS
Casa Montaña
Calle Jose Benlliure, 69
46011 El Cabanyal
96-367-2314
www.emilianobodega.com
Classic recipes, made with modern refinements.
Wonderful wines.

La Matandeta
Carretera Alfafar El Saler, km 4
46910 Alfafar
96-211-21-84
Go for the paella.

VALLADOLID HOTELS
Hotel Zenit Imperial
Calle del Paso, 4
983-330-300
www.himperial.com
Perfect location in the center of the city and
helpful staff.

AC Palacio de Santa Ana
Calle Santa Ana
www.ac-hotels.com
983-409-920
A short drive from the city center, this hotel used to
be a convent and it's quite beautiful.

Parador de Tordesillas
Carretera de Salamanca, 5
47100 Tordesillas
983-770-051
www.parador.es
The landscape is quite serene and beautiful, . . . and
there's golf!

VALLADOLID RESTAURANTS
La Criolla
Calle Fernández de la Torre, 2
983-373-822
www.restaurantelacriolla.es
Have the lechazo, of course, and a bottle of the
Vega Sicilia if you can.

La Corte
Paseo Zorrilla, 10
983-338-785
In the center of town, this has great old-fashioned
Castilian food in a modern building.

La Parrilla de San Lorenzo
Calle Pedro Niño, 1
983-335-088
The restaurant used to be a monastery, and it
honors Saint Lawrence who, as the story goes, was
martyred on a parrilla, an iron grill. (Supposedly
he told his torturer when it was time to turn him
over—eek!)

Mesón Cervantes
Calle de Rastro, 6
983-308-810
A local favorite. Try the river crabs if they are in
season and the veal Don Quixote–style.

VIC RESTAURANT
Can Jubany
Carretera de Sant Hilari
08506 Calldetenes
93-889-10-23
www.canjubany.com
Go to this restaurant soon, before it gets too hard
to get into!

VITORIA HOTELS
Gran Hotel Lakua
Calle Tarragona, 8
945-181-000
www.granhotelakua.com
Located in the Lakua area of Vitoria, this hotel
is very convenient for a road-tripper, since it's
connected with the main road.

Hotel General Álava
Avenida Gasteiz, 79
945-21-50-00
www.hga.info
Right in the middle of the city and recently
renovated.

VITORIA RESTAURANTS
Asador Sagartoki
Calle del Prado, 18
945-288-676
A must-go kind of place—Senén's food is
intelligent, delicious, and memorable.

Restaurant Etxebarri
Plaza San Juan, 1
48291 Axpe-Marzana, Atxondo
94-658-3042
www.asadoretxebarri.com
Grilling at its finest.

Index

FOOD, RECIPES, & COOKING TECHNIQUES

(Page references in *italic* refer to photographs of foods and recipes.)

PEOPLE & PLACES